The
BROWNIE
EXPERIENCE

The BROWNIE EXPERIENCE

...a cookbook for brownie~lovers

RECIPES, ILLUSTRATIONS, CALLIGRAPHY,
and HAND~LETTERING

by

Lisa Tanner

TEN SPEED PRESS
Berkeley, California

1◉
TEN SPEED PRESS
P.O. Box 7123
Berkeley, California 94707

Library of Congress Catalog Number: 84~50926
ISBN: 0~89815~135~X

Cover illustration by Lisa Tanner

Printed in the United States of America
10 9 8 7 6 5 4 3 2

To my father, Leonard Wolfson, who in the short time that I knew him inspired me to do many things, and to be all I can be in this life. His appreciation of the little things ~ such as food ~ certainly did rub off on his daughters. And here lie the results. Thank you, Daddy.

Acknowledgments:

I wish to thank several special brownie fans for helpfully partaking in this venture of mine.

First, my sister Roberta, for patiently typing the manuscript, and for strongly believing in this project from the very beginning. Second, my loving husband Paul, who lugged oversized platters of brownies to his firestation at 5:45 am and never once complained. Third, my mother Marian, who happily babysat, giving me time in which to work.

Special heartfelt thanks to the sweet~toothed firemen of Station #47 (L. A. City) for consuming and criticizing brownie after brownie after brownie, and to my supportive friends: Lisa, Mary, Lynn, Cheryl, Robyn, Judi, Terry and Anna Banana ♥ who always believed in me and gave me heartwarming encouragement in pursuing my dreams. And to anyone else who taste~tested and gained a pound here and there in the process ... I thank you all.

A Brownie Introduction

In these days of health and nutrition consciousness, why did I choose to write a cookbook about brownies? I firmly believe there comes a time in one's daily life when healthful routines must be broken. There's a devil in each of us that must break the rules and consume a forbidden sweet once in awhile. And if one is going to indulge, why let it be anything other than the very best? I ask you, what is more desirable than an outrageously delicious brownie filled with delights such as toasted coconut, chocolate chips, sweet cherries, or macadamia nuts? And that's only a small sample of what is yet to come, so read on!

No, this isn't an ordinary cookbook. It's a collection of very unique and original brownie recipes simple enough to whip up for friends or for brown bag lunches, but elegant enough to serve to your most discriminating dinner guests on your finest china. They will undoubtedly swoon with passion over your brownie creations.

You ask, "How can such simple things bring so much enjoyment?" I think I have the answer... and that is precisely why this book was written.

Lisa Tanner

Table of Contents

PAGE

WHAT IS A BROWNIE ? 11

TASTE TESTING 13

USING REAL INGREDIENTS 14

BAKING AHEAD 17

DOUBLING OR HALVING A RECIPE 18

ABOUT UTENSILS 19

A FEW WORDS ABOUT FROSTINGS AND GARNISHES 20

THE BROWNIE RECIPE COLLECTION 21

CHOCOLATE~IN~THE~BATTER BROWNIES 22

LUSCIOUS NO~BAKE BROWNIES 55

CHOCOLATE~CHIPPED BROWNIES 64

continued...

	PAGE
CHOCOLATE~LESS BROWNIES	78
HEALTH CONSCIOUS BROWNIES	105
ELEGANT AND EXOTIC BROWNIES	122
BROWNIE CREATIONS AND SPECIALTIES	138
FROZEN BROWNIE~WICHES	139
SHAPELY BROWNIE CELEBRATIONS!	142
THE BROWNIE SUNDAE	144
THE BROWNIE BANANA SPLIT	145
BROWNIE MUD PIE	148
PARFAITS AND GOBLETS	151
DO-IT-YOURSELF BROWNIE SUNDAE BUFFET	154
THE BROWNIE ORGY EXPERIENCE	158
SOME SUGGESTED FRUITS, SAUCES AND TOPPINGS	162
INDEX	165

What is a Brownie?

All this talk of brownies, and I've yet to even define the term. According to the thickest, most popular dictionary, a brownie can be one of four things. 1) From folklore, "A small, good natured goblin believed to perform helpful domestic services at night." 2) "A junior Girl Scout, between the ages of 7 and 9." 3) "A flat, moist cakelike chocolate cookie containing nuts." 4) From Australia, "A rough sweetened cake made with currants."

This book isn't about goblins or Girl Scouts or even Australian cakes, so I suppose that leaves us to explore definition #3. After doing my research on "The Brownie" with all its variations, I put together this (moderately elaborate) definition. Here goes... Brown~ie (brou'nē) n. A cross between a cookie and a cake, some~ times containing nuts or other crunchy morsels; can be chewy or caky or fluffy; thin or thick; frosted or plain; baked or unbaked; and (finally) cut into bars, squares, or other interesting shapes.

As you gaze through the recipes in this book, you will notice that most include chocolate in one form or another. Some even include two different types of chocolate to satisfy the most persis~ tent craving. And some recipes use no chocolate at all, but I still call them brownies. They boast the same rich texture and su~ perb taste without containing even a speck of chocolate. Try them, you won't be disappointed. These unchocolate brownies are not a typical bar cookie consisting of a sweet crust and a poured-on topping. They are genuine chewy, caky, fudgy brownies with a base other than chocolate... maybe butterscotch, peanut butter or pumpkin.

One thing all brownies do have in common is their ability to spread sweet enjoyment among those who consume them. Watch everyone's face light up with pleasure as you approach them with a platterful of your favorite recipe. To offer someone a homemade brownie is like offering a bit of Grandma's kitchen, a bit of kindness and love.

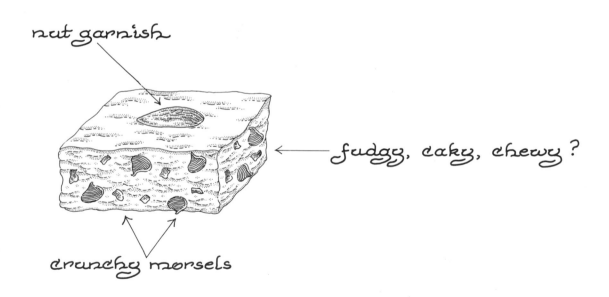

nut garnish

fudgy, caky, chewy?

crunchy morsels

Taste Testing

Who is qualified to taste test a brownie? Or better yet, who isn't? There are no brownie experts, only brownie-lovers. We all have our preferences. Some of us like fudgy brownies, while others prefer theirs on the caky side. Some love walnuts, others almonds. And there are some who love their brownies frosted in chocolate or under a big pile of ice cream.

There is no right or wrong in the world of brownies. But there are certain select individuals who may be better qualified, if by only a slight margin, to judge what are really the "best." These are people who have an unusual lust for sweets—not Twinkies, but something unique and luscious. Something worth spending some serious calories on. These people became my critics.

Each brownie recipe in this book has been sampled, revised, then re-sampled perhaps several times to achieve just the right proportion of nuts or chocolate or eggs. My oven stayed hot for months. Firemen, home-makers, children, grandmas, daddies—they all tasted and tasted and tasted. I baked hundreds of brownies in my kitchen; the ones described on these pages are the cream of the crop. Each contains only the highest quality ingredients, and each has its own unique flavor combination. They are so fabulous, I was tempted to keep some of them secret. But instead, I share them with you, my toughest critics. And I'm sure you'll agree with me, from the moment you taste test your first batch, that these are not ordinary brownies, these are extraordinary treats—sweets to remember, and to enjoy with great enthusiasm.

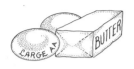
Using Real Ingredients

You may notice as you breeze through this book, I list only the "real McCoy" of ingredients in my recipes. What I mean is...no margarine, imitation vanilla, generic chocolate chips, or vegetable shortening. You may as well stop at a bakery or resort to a brownie mix. To get real taste you need to bake with honest~to~goodness ingredients—pure butter, real chocolate, unprocessed flours and nuts, and fresh whole eggs. Imitations just won't do, not when it comes to baking something worthwhile. You are not fooling anyone when you substitute an inferior ingredient. The results just won't be the same. Remember, you deserve only the best.

SOME BASIC BROWNIE~BAKING INGREDIENTS

- **BANANAS** ~ use the ripest possible.
- **BUTTER** ~ to soften, let sticks warm to room temperature.
- **BUTTERSCOTCH CHIPS** ~ a wonderful invention. Sold like chocolate chips.
- **CAROB CHIPS** ~ sold in bulk or sealed packages at most health food stores are a tasty addition to many of those "Health Conscious" brownie recipes. (Also good eaten out of hand.)
- **CHOCOLATE** ~ use the real thing.
    <u>Chocolate chips</u> ~ both milk and semi~sweet. Use semi~sweet

unless milk chocolate is called for in the recipe.

Unsweetened chocolate squares ~ sold in 8~oz. boxes. Each ounce is individually wrapped for convenience.

White chocolate ~ sold in stars or blocks in candy depart~ ments. Be careful to use a double boiler or very low heat to melt.

∽ COCOA POWDER ~ unsweetened only!

∽ COCONUT ~ flaked, shredded, or chips. To toast: place coconut in a single layer on a pan in a 350° oven until golden, stirring occasionally.

∽ CREAM CHEESE ~ sold in 3~oz. or 8~oz. packages.

∽ DRIED FRUIT ~ dates, apricots, raisins, etc. To chop, use a very sharp knife or scissors dipped periodically in hot water to con~ trol stickiness.

∽ EGGS ~ large AA.

∽ FLOUR ~ read labels, please.

Unbleached white flour ~ use when just "flour" is called for in a recipe.

Whole wheat pastry flour ~ this is a lighter flour than traditional whole wheat flour, and gives excellent results in brownie~baking. Using regular whole wheat flour will yield a heavier textured brownie, since more of the coarser grain still remains. You can sift, then measure whole wheat flour for a lighter product, or use it in combination with unbleached white flour.

∽ GRAHAM CRACKER CRUMBS ~ you can buy a box of already

crushed crumbs or crush your own in a blender. And don't forget the whole wheat variety found in natural food stores and some supermarkets. They're delicious, and make especially tasty brownies.

↪ HONEY ~ use a pure, light honey (for example, orange honey). The taste is sweet, delicate, and not overpowering. If you do a lot of "Health Conscious" baking, buy a large 5-pound can, and for heaven's sake, keep the rim clean!

↪ LIQUEURS ~ coffee, cherry, mint, almond, chocolate.

↪ MARSHMALLOWS ~ use miniature ones.

↪ NUTS ~ both raw and toasted. Toast on a cookie sheet in a 350° oven until lightly brown and crisp. For ground nuts, process at high speed in a blender until powdery.

↪ PEANUT BUTTER ~ pure and smooth, without preservatives.

↪ PEANUT BUTTER CHIPS ~ a delicious brownie-baking addition.

↪ SUGAR ~ both granulated and brown.

↪ SWEETENED CONDENSED MILK ~ sold in 14-oz. cans. (Do not use evaporated milk.) A must for no-bake brownies.

↪ VANILLA EXTRACT ~ pure only, please. Ditto for almond, maple, lemon, etc.

↪ VANILLA WAFER CRUMBS ~ buy a box of vanilla wafers, crumble into a blender and process. To measure, be sure to pack down crumbs if the recipe calls for it.

⌠ Baking Ahead ⌠

All the brownies in this book can be frozen with excellent results, except for Chocolate Kahlúa Mousse Brownies. They are a little too fine~textured and delicate to be frozen. However, they store quite well, covered, in the refrigerator. In fact, all these brownies may safely sit in your refrigerator several days (provided they are covered), and some even taste better this way. So bake ahead, store some brownies in your freezer or refrigerator, and you'll be ready for pop~in guests (it's nice to be able to serve a plateful of delicious homemade brownies on the spur of the moment), for a party (bake several different kinds of brownies and freeze them to avoid any last minute fuss or a hot kitchen), or to whip up any of the marvelous desserts described on the pages to come (ice cream bars, sundaes and parfaits are all made in minutes once you've done a little homework).

To freeze brownies, simply wrap them tightly in foil with a layer of plastic wrap between bars to inhibit sticking. Or use plas~tic bags. For the extra~fudgy types, you may wish to freeze them unwrapped on a waxed paper~lined cookie sheet. Put them in plastic bags or wrap them in foil once they are frozen solid. Thaw frozen brownies at room temperature for an hour or so, sift on some powdered sugar if you wish, or swirl on a favorite frosting. No one will know they were even frozen.

You may find it easier to freeze the uncut brownie by cooling it thoroughly in the pan and wrapping in a double piece of aluminum foil, sealing well. Thaw at room temperature about an hour or until bar softens just enough to cut into squares with a sharp knife. You'll get very clean edges this way, and it will be easier to cut through chocolate chips or nuts.

∽ Doubling or Halving a Recipe ∽

Most of the recipes in this book can be doubled without too much of a problem. You can easily double a brownie recipe and freeze the extra batch for a surprise dessert in the future (something to look forward to!), so as long as you're in the mood, why not bake a little extra? Recipes can also be halved, but this could be trickier, especially if the recipe calls for a measurement of ⅓ cup of honey or a can of sweetened condensed milk. Whatever you do, remember to make measurements as precise as possible, and remember to take pan size into consideration. Listed below are some substitutions:

1 (13 x 9 x 2") pan ≈ 2 (8" or 9") square pans

1 (8" or 9") pan ≈ 2 (9 x 5 x 3") loaf pans

For example: cut a recipe using an 8" or 9" pan in half and bake in a loaf pan. Or double an 8" or 9" recipe and use a

18

13 x 9 x 2" pan. When doubling or halving, check brownies for doneness a few minutes before the allotted time, just in case.

Incidentally, if you use Pyrex dishes instead of tin, lower your oven temperature by 25°.

∾ About Utensils ∾

A beater... a whisk... a wooden spoon?

Some recipes specify what tool you should use for creaming, folding, stirring or beating. Whenever possible, I use a wire whisk to cream ingredients together, provided the butter is soft and the batter doesn't require a lengthy beating. It's also a good tool for mixing ingredients together quickly and thoroughly with a few swift strokes. If a wire whisk is called for in the recipe, the batter doesn't require a beater, but a spoon won't be quite tough enough.

When a beater is specified, you can be sure it's necessary. For heavy batters that need lots of creaming, or for whipping up egg whites, you'll need a hand or electric beater—whichever is handy.

You can use a wooden spoon or rubber spatula for stirring, adding ingredients, or folding it all together. But beware, I've broken countless rubber spatulas with stiff batters. Trust your instincts and your own good judgement.

19

A Few Words About Frostings and Garnishes

Only a few of the brownie recipes in this book call for a frosting. The reason is this: most of the brownies are so delicious and flavorful they simply don't need a fancy, gooey topping. When a frosting recipe is given with the brownie, you can be sure their flavors enhance each other, and that they taste best together. But feel free to experiment on your own.

Powdered sugar sifted over the top of the brownie makes a wonderful garnish. It's decorative without being heavy or too sweet. Nuts (whole, chopped or ground) or coconut (plain or toasted) follow close behind as exceptional garnishes. They add wholesomeness and a delightful crunch.

Here's a tip to follow: never overpower the taste and texture of your brownies with anything overly sweet or heavy. If a garnish or a frosting masks even a little of the brownie's character, it isn't subtle enough. Opt instead for just a light dusting of powdered sugar, or nothing at all. If you do use frosting, put on a thin layer, and let the brownie itself dominate.

The Brownie RECIPE COLLECTION

...DIVIDED INTO 6 DELECTABLE SECTIONS:

PAGE

Chocolate~in~the~Batter Brownies 22

Luscious No~Bake Brownies 55

Chocolate~Chipped Brownies 64

Chocolate~Less Brownies 78

Health Conscious Brownies 105

Elegant and Exotic Brownies 122

CHOCOLATE~IN~THE~BATTER BROWNIES

When most of us think of brownies, we think of chocolate. This chapter is devoted to making the ordinary but lovable chocolate brownie incredibly tempting by adding some creative touches: sweet liqueurs, nutty toppings, fruits, spices, and much, much more!

⌁ Sour Cream Chocolate Chip Brownies ⌁

Very light, very moist, very tender ~ and very good!

½ cup butter, softened
1 cup sugar
1 egg
1 cup sour cream
1 teaspoon vanilla
2 cups flour
½ cup unsweetened cocoa
½ teaspoon baking soda
½ teaspoon salt
1 cup chopped chocolate chips

~ powdered sugar ~

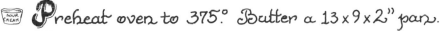

Preheat oven to 375°. Butter a 13 x 9 x 2" pan.

In a large bowl, using a wire whisk, cream together butter and sugar. Beat in egg, then sour cream and vanilla. In a small bowl, stir together flour, cocoa, baking soda and salt. Gradually blend dry ingredients into creamed mixture; mix well. Fold in chocolate chips. Batter will be fairly stiff. Spread in pan.

Bake 20~25 minutes, or until toothpick inserted in center comes out clean. Cool completely in pan.

Sift powdered sugar over top, and cut into bars.

Makes 32 brownies

～ Chocolate Caramel Turtle Brownies ～

A chocolate brownie base with a baked~on candy~like topping. Scrumptious!

¼ cup butter
2 oz. unsweetened chocolate
2 eggs
1 cup sugar
¼ teaspoon salt
½ teaspoon vanilla
½ cup flour

½ cup pecan halves
Caramel Syrup (recipe follows)
¾ cup chocolate chips

Preheat oven to 350°. Butter an 8" square pan.

In a small saucepan, melt butter and unsweetened chocolate together over low heat; set aside. In a medium~sized bowl, beat eggs with wire whisk; beat until light. Beat in sugar, salt and vanilla until blended. Stir in chocolate mixture, then flour. Pour into pan.

Bake 15 minutes. Meanwhile, prepare Caramel Syrup.

Carefully remove pan from oven and sprinkle top evenly with pecans. Gently top pecans with cooked Caramel Syrup, covering surface completely.

Bake 15 minutes longer, or until caramel is bubbling over entire top of brownie. Remove from oven and immediately sprinkle with chocolate chips. Let chocolate melt slightly, then _very_ gently swirl surface with a knife.

Cool completely before cutting. Chill to harden chocolate if necessary. Serve at room temperature.

Makes 24 brownies.

Caramel Syrup

½ cup butter
⅓ cup brown sugar, lightly packed

Bring butter and sugar to a boil in a small saucepan, stirring constantly. Stir and simmer one minute.

Double Chocolate Peanut Brownies

Really fudgy, with chocolate chips and toasted peanuts pressed on top for extra crunch.

½ cup butter
2 oz. unsweetened chocolate
1 cup sugar
1 egg
½ teaspoon vanilla
½ cup flour
⅓ cup chopped toasted peanuts
⅓ cup chocolate chips

Preheat oven to 350°. Lightly butter an 8" square pan.

In a small saucepan, melt butter and chocolate together over low heat. Remove from heat and beat in sugar, then egg and vanilla. Stir in flour until well combined. Spread in pan. Combine peanuts and chocolate chips; sprinkle evenly over top of batter, pressing down lightly.

Bake about 35 minutes, or until top springs back when lightly pressed with fingertip.

Cool completely in pan. Cut into squares.

Makes 16 brownies

Mandarin Chocolate Chip Brownies

A splendid combination of orange, dark chocolate and toasty almonds.

¼ cup butter
2 oz. unsweetened chocolate
2 eggs
1 cup sugar
2 tablespoons frozen orange juice concentrate, thawed
1 rounded teaspoon grated orange rind
¼ teaspoon salt
½ teaspoon vanilla
½ cup flour
½ cup chopped, toasted almonds
¼ cup chopped chocolate chips

Preheat oven to 350°. Lightly butter an 8" square pan.

Melt together butter and chocolate; cool. In a medium~sized bowl, beat eggs until light. Beat in sugar, orange concentrate, orange rind, salt and vanilla. Stir in cooled chocolate mixture. Blend in flour. Fold in nuts and chocolate chips. Pour into pan.

Bake 30 minutes, or until toothpick inserted in center comes out clean.

Cool in pan before cutting. These brownies age well.

Makes 16 brownies

Zucchini Nut Brownies

Moist texture; lightly spiced; delicate chocolate flavor.

¼ cup butter
2 oz. unsweetened chocolate
2 eggs
1 cup sugar
¼ teaspoon salt
½ teaspoon vanilla
¾ cup flour
½ teaspoon each cinnamon
and allspice

¼ teaspoon each nutmeg and ginger
½ cup packed finely grated zucchini
(squeezed dry)
½ cup chopped walnuts
½ cup chopped raisins or currants

~ powdered sugar ~

Preheat oven to 350.° Butter an 8" square pan.

Over low heat, melt together butter and chocolate; set aside. In a medium~sized bowl, using a wire whisk, beat eggs until foamy. Beat in sugar, salt and vanilla. Stir in melted chocolate mixture. In a small bowl, combine flour and spices. Gradually stir dry ingredients into chocolate mixture, blending well. Thoroughly fold in zucchini, walnuts and raisins. Spread batter evenly in pan.

Bake 20~25 minutes, or until toothpick inserted in center comes out clean.

Cool completely. Dust with powdered sugar, and cut into squares.

Makes 16 brownies.

Chocolate Amaretto Crunch Brownies

Its moistness comes from ground almonds, brown sugar, and almond liqueur. Excellent chilled.

2 cups whole blanched almonds
4 eggs, room temperature
1½ cups brown sugar, packed
⅔ cup unsweetened cocoa
1 cup minus 2 tablespoons flour
½ teaspoon salt
¼ cup Amaretto
1 cup chocolate chips

~ powdered sugar ~

- **P**reheat oven to 350°. Butter a 13 x 9 x 2" pan.

- **G**rind nuts to a powder in blender; set aside. In a large bowl, beat eggs well with wire whisk. Add sugar and beat until thick. In another bowl, mix together cocoa, flour, salt and ground almonds; stir into creamed mixture until well combined. Blend in Amaretto and chocolate chips. Spread in pan.

- **B**ake 20~25 minutes, or until toothpick inserted in center comes out clean.

- **C**ool completely. Sift powdered sugar over top and cut into bars.

Makes 32 brownies.

～ Chocolate Mint Brownies ～

Thin, crunchy brownie bars, frosted with creamy mint and drizzled with sweet chocolate.

2 oz. unsweetened chocolate
½ cup butter
2 eggs
1 cup brown sugar, lightly packed
½ cup flour
½ cup sliced almonds
Peppermint Cream Frosting
Sweet Chocolate Glaze

○ **P**reheat oven to 350.° Butter a 9" square pan.

○ **M**elt chocolate and butter together over low heat; cool. In a medium~ sized bowl, beat together sugar and eggs until very creamy. Stir in choc~ olate mixture, then flour and almonds. Blend well. Pour into pan.

○ **B**ake 25~30 minutes, or until toothpick inserted in center comes out clean. Cool completely.

○ **S**pread Peppermint Cream Frosting over uncut brownies. Chill until firm. With a spatula or knife, drizzle Sweet Chocolate Glaze in a criss~

cross pattern over frosting.

⬭ Chill again, then cut into sticks. Store in refrigerator.

Makes 24 brownies.

Peppermint Cream Frosting

1 ½ cups powdered sugar
3 tablespoons butter, softened
2 tablespoons milk
½ teaspoon peppermint extract
2 drops green food coloring

⬭ Blend together all ingredients except food coloring until smooth and creamy. Stir in enough food coloring to tint a pale mint green; blend well.

Sweet Chocolate Glaze

2 oz. semi~sweet chocolate
2 tablespoons butter

⬭ Melt together over low heat, stirring until smooth.

Yogurt Almond Brownies

Very moist, with a delicate chocolate almond flavor.

3 oz. unsweetened chocolate
1 cup flour
½ teaspoon baking powder
½ teaspoon salt
¼ teaspoon baking soda
½ cup plus 2 tablespoons butter, softened
1¼ cups brown sugar, lightly packed

3 eggs
1¼ teaspoons vanilla
¼ teaspoon almond extract
1 cup plain yogurt, room temperature
⅔ cup finely chopped almonds
1 cup chopped chocolate chips
~ ⅓ cup finely chopped almonds ~ (for topping)

Preheat oven to 350°. Butter a 13 x 9 x 2" pan.

Melt chocolate over low heat; cool. In a small bowl, stir together flour, baking powder, salt and baking soda. In a large bowl, with electric mixer, cream together butter and sugar until light and fluffy. Beat in eggs, one at a time. Add vanilla and almond extracts. Alternately blend yogurt and flour mixture into creamed mixture. Stir in cooled chocolate, ⅔ cup almonds and chocolate chips. Pour into pan. Sprinkle top with re~ maining ⅓ cup chopped almonds.

Bake about 40 minutes, or until toothpick comes out clean. Cool before cutting into bars.

Makes 32 brownies.

Fudgy Raspberry Brownies

Dark and devilish!

6 oz. unsweetened chocolate
1 cup butter
2 cups sugar
4 eggs
2 teaspoons vanilla

1½ cups flour
½ teaspoon each baking powder
　and salt
1 cup sliced almonds
1 cup milk chocolate chips
¾ cup raspberry preserves

Preheat oven to 350.° Lightly butter a 13 x 9 x 2" pan.

In a medium~sized saucepan, over low heat, melt together unsweetened chocolate and butter, stirring often. Remove from heat. With wire whisk, beat in sugar, eggs and vanilla. Transfer mixture to a large bowl and cool slightly. Gradually stir in flour, baking powder and salt just to combine. Fold in almonds and chocolate chips. Spread about ¾ of batter evenly in pan. Carefully spread raspberry preserves on top of batter. Drizzle remaining batter evenly over preserves swirling top lightly with a spoon. Gently smooth top.

Bake 20~25 minutes, or until top is firm and toothpick inserted in center comes out clean.

Cool completely before cutting.

Makes 32 brownies.

Note: For Fudgy Strawberry Brownies, simply substitute strawberry preserves.

33

Spicy Chocolate Chip Brownies

Moist with molasses, chewy with raisins, spiced with orange.

2 oz. unsweetened chocolate
¼ cup butter
⅓ cup molasses
½ cup brown sugar, lightly packed
1 teaspoon grated orange rind
1 egg
1 cup flour

1 teaspoon baking powder
½ teaspoon cinnamon
¼ teaspoon each allspice, cloves and salt
½ cup raisins
½ cup chopped chocolate chips
~ powdered sugar ~

Preheat oven to 350.° Butter a 9" square pan.

Melt chocolate and butter together over low heat; set aside. In a medium-sized bowl, using a wire whisk, blend together molasses, sugar and orange rind. Beat in egg, then chocolate mixture. In a separate bowl, stir together flour and remaining ingredients except raisins and chocolate chips. Gradually blend dry ingredients into chocolate mixture. Stir in raisins and chocolate chips; mix well. Turn batter into pan.

Bake 20 minutes, or until toothpick inserted in center comes out clean. Cool in pan on wire rack.

Lightly sift powdered sugar over top before cutting into bars.
Makes 20 brownies.

Ultimate Fudge Brownies

Bet you can't eat just one!

5 oz. unsweetened chocolate
1 cup butter, softened
1 ¾ cups brown sugar, packed
5 eggs
1½ teaspoons vanilla
1 cup flour
1 cup coarsely chopped pecans
~ powdered sugar ~

Preheat oven to 350.° Butter a 13 x 9 x 2" pan.

Melt chocolate; set aside to cool. With wire whisk or hand mixer, cream together butter and sugar. Beat in eggs, one at a time. Add vanilla. Blend in melted chocolate, then flour. Stir in pecans. Spread mixture in pan.

Bake 20~30 minutes, or until toothpick inserted in center comes out clean. Cool in pan.

Sift powdered sugar lightly over top before cutting into bars.
Makes 32 brownies.

Fudgy Macadamia Nut Brownies

Pure paradise.

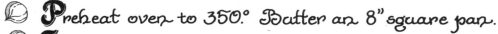

3 oz. unsweetened chocolate
½ cup butter
1 cup sugar
2 eggs
1 teaspoon vanilla

¾ cup flour
¼ teaspoon baking powder
¼ teaspoon salt
1¼ cups chopped toasted macadamia nuts

Preheat oven to 350.° Butter an 8" square pan.

In a medium~sized saucepan, melt chocolate and butter together over very low heat, stirring occasionally. Remove from heat. Beat in sugar, eggs and vanilla. Stir in flour, baking powder and salt just until thoroughly moistened. Fold in 1 cup of the nuts. Spread mixture in pan. Sprinkle top evenly with remaining ¼ cup of nuts.

Bake 20~25 minutes. Do not overbake.

Cool completely in pan on wire rack. Cut into squares with a sharp knife.

Makes 16 brownies.

Variation: For even richer brownies, substitute ½ cup chocolate chips for ½ cup of the macadamias in the batter. Sprinkle top with ¼ cup more nuts, as directed above.

Mocha Almond Fudge Brownies

Probably the best brownies you will ever encounter.

5 oz. unsweetened chocolate
1 rounded tablespoon powdered instant coffee
1 cup butter, softened
1 ¾ cups brown sugar, packed
5 eggs
1 ½ teaspoons vanilla
1 cup flour
1 cup chopped, toasted almonds
½ cup chopped chocolate chips

Preheat oven to 350.° Butter a 13 x 9 x 2" pan.

Melt chocolate over low heat; stir in coffee powder and let cool. In a large bowl, with wire whisk, cream together butter and sugar. Add eggs, one at a time, beating well after each. Blend in vanilla, then melted chocolate mixture. Grad~ually stir in flour. Fold in almonds and chocolate chips. Spread batter in pan.

Bake 20 ~ 30 minutes, or until done. Let cool in pan completely before cut ~ ting.

Makes 32 brownies.

Optional, but NICE garnish: Sliced almonds pressed onto top before baking. They get toasty and delicious!

Coconut Marshmallow Creme Brownies

A brownie to satisfy your sweet tooth.

3/4 cup butter, melted
1½ cups sugar
1 teaspoon vanilla
3 eggs
½ cup unsweetened cocoa
3/4 teaspoon baking powder
¼ teaspoon salt
1 cup flour
½ cup coconut
½ cup chopped pecans
⅓ cup chopped milk chocolate chips

1 cup marshmallow creme
Chocolate Cream Frosting (recipe follows)
~ ¼ cup additional coconut ~

Preheat oven to 350.° Butter a 9" square pan.

In a large bowl, beat together butter and sugar using a wire whisk. Blend in vanilla. Beat in eggs one at a time until creamy. Stir in cocoa, baking powder, salt and flour; mix well. Stir in ½ cup coconut, pecans and choc~

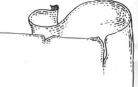

...olate chips. Pour into pan.

- 🥫 **B**ake about 35 minutes, or until toothpick inserted in center comes out clean. Remove from oven and gently spread marshmallow creme evenly over hot brownie layer.

- 🥫 **P**repare Chocolate Cream Frosting. Spread over warm marshmallow creme. Swirl together with a knife to marbleize. Sprinkle top with remaining ¼ cup coconut.

- 🥫 **C**ool completely in pan. Chill, then cut into bars.

Makes 20 brownies.

Chocolate Cream Frosting

2 tablespoons butter, melted
1 tablespoon plus 1½ teaspoons unsweetened cocoa
1 cup powdered sugar
¼ teaspoon vanilla

- 🥫 **B**lend together all ingredients in a small bowl until creamy.

Chocolate Peanut Butter Chip Brownies

A rich, yummy combination of peanut butter and chocolate.

2 oz. unsweetened chocolate
¼ cup butter, softened
¼ cup peanut butter
1 cup brown sugar, lightly packed
2 eggs
1 teaspoon vanilla
½ cup flour
1 heaping cup peanut butter chips

🥜 **P**reheat oven to 325°. Lightly butter an 8" square pan.

🥜 **M**elt chocolate over low heat; set aside to cool. In a medium~sized bowl, cream together butter, peanut butter and brown sugar, using wire whisk. Beat in eggs and vanilla. Mix in melted chocolate. Blend in flour and chips. Pour into pan.

🥜 **B**ake 30~35 minutes, or until edges begin to leave sides of pan.

🥜 **C**ool completely before cutting.

Makes 16 brownies.

Banana Chocolate Chip Brownies

Thick and moist. Tastes like a chocolate~dipped banana.

¾ cup flour
¼ teaspoon baking soda
¼ teaspoon salt
⅓ cup butter
¾ cup brown sugar, lightly packed
1½ cups chocolate chips (divided)

1 teaspoon vanilla
2 eggs
1 small very ripe banana, mashed (½ cup)
½ cup chopped walnuts
~powdered sugar~

Preheat oven to 325°. Butter a 9" square pan.

In a small bowl, stir together flour, baking soda and salt; set aside. In a small saucepan, combine butter and brown sugar. Bring to a boil over low heat, stirring constantly. Immediately remove from heat and stir in 1 cup of the chocolate chips until melted and smooth. Blend in vanilla. Transfer mixture to a large mix~ing bowl and cool slightly. With wire whisk, beat in eggs one at a time. Blend in mashed banana, then flour mixture. Fold in remaining ½ cup chocolate chips and walnuts. Spread in pan.

Bake about 45 minutes. Cool completely in pan.

Lightly sift powdered sugar over top before cutting into bars.

Makes 20 brownies.

∽ Fudgy Fruitcake Brownies ∾

Spiked with brandy, and full of holiday surprises.

3 oz. unsweetened chocolate
½ cup butter
1 cup brown sugar, packed
2 eggs
1 teaspoon vanilla
2 tablespoons brandy
¾ cup flour
¼ teaspoon baking powder

¼ teaspoon salt
½ cup red and green candied cherries,
 quartered
½ cup each chopped pecans and golden raisins
½ cup chopped candied pineapple
∽ powdered sugar ∾
∽ 10 candied cherries, halved ∾

Preheat oven to 350.° Butter a 9" square pan.

In a large saucepan over low heat, melt together chocolate and butter. Remove from heat. With wire whisk, beat in sugar and eggs. Stir in vanilla and brandy. Blend in flour, baking powder and salt. Fold in cherries, pecans, raisins and pineapple. Mix gently but thoroughly. Pour into pan.

Bake 30~35 minutes, or until toothpick inserted in center comes out clean.

Cool completely in pan. Sift powdered sugar over top. Cut into bars, and decorate each one with a candied cherry half.

Makes 20 brownies.

White Chocolate Chip Brownies

Buttery chocolate bars with flecks of white chocolate throughout. Marvelous!

1 cup semi~sweet chocolate chips
2 cups vanilla wafer crumbs, lightly packed
1 14~oz. can sweetened condensed milk
1 teaspoon vanilla
1 cup coarsely chopped white chocolate

Preheat oven to 350°. Lightly butter a 9" square pan.

Melt semi~sweet chocolate chips over low heat until smooth; set aside to cool completely. In a medium~sized bowl, stir together vanilla wafer crumbs and sweetened condensed milk. Thoroughly blend in melted chocolate and vanilla. Stir in chopped white chocolate; mix well. Turn batter into pan.

Bake 25~30 minutes, or until firm and toothpick inserted in center comes out clean.

Cool and cut into bars.

Makes 20 brownies.

Chocolate Butterscotch Swirl Brownies

Marbled chocolate and butterscotch batters. Pecans for crunch.

1 cup chocolate chips
1 cup butterscotch chips
2 cups flour
1½ teaspoons baking powder
½ teaspoon salt

1 cup butter, softened
1 cup brown sugar, packed
2 teaspoons vanilla
3 eggs
1 cup chopped pecans

Preheat oven to 350°. Butter a 13 x 9 x 2" pan.

Melt chocolate and butterscotch chips <u>separately</u> over very low heat; set mixtures aside. In a small bowl, stir together flour, baking powder and salt. In a large bowl, combine butter, brown sugar and vanilla; beat until creamy. Add eggs one at a time, beating well after each. Gradually stir in flour mixture, then pecans. Divide batter in half. Blend melted butterscotch chips into one half of batter. To remaining batter, thoroughly stir in melted chocolate. In pan, alternate "globs" of butterscotch and chocolate batters checkerboard fashion until both mixtures are used. Swirl together with a knife to marbleize. Gently smooth top of batter with a wet hand to make an even layer.

Bake about 35 minutes, or until done.

Cool completely in pan before cutting into bars.

Makes 32 brownies.

Chocolate Pudding Brownies

These may very well become your favorite. Moist,
with exceptional chocolate flavor.

¾ cup butter, melted and cooled
1 cup sugar
1 teaspoon vanilla
¼ teaspoon salt
3 eggs
½ cup unsweetened cocoa
¾ teaspoon baking powder
1 cup flour
½ cup dry chocolate pudding and pie filling mix (not instant)
½ heaping cup milk chocolate chips

Preheat oven to 350°. Butter a 9" square pan.

In a large bowl, combine melted butter and sugar. With wire whisk, beat until well blended. Beat in vanilla, salt and eggs. Blend in cocoa, baking powder, flour and pudding mix. Stir in chocolate chips. Pour into pan.

Bake 25~30 minutes, or until toothpick inserted in center comes out clean.

Cool completely in pan before cutting into bars.

Makes 20 brownies.

Cream Cheese Swirl Brownies

Moist and fudgy, with a luscious cream cheese ribbon.

3 tablespoons butter
4 oz. semi~sweet chocolate, or ⅔ cup semi~sweet chocolate chips
2 tablespoons butter, softened
1 3oz. package cream cheese, softened
¼ cup sugar
1 egg
1 tablespoon flour
1 teaspoon vanilla

2 eggs
¾ cup sugar
½ cup flour
½ teaspoon each baking powder and salt
1 teaspoon vanilla
½ cup chopped blanched almonds
¼ teaspoon almond extract

 Preheat oven to 350°. Butter a 9" square pan.

 Melt together 3 tablespoons butter and chocolate over low heat; set aside to cool. Using electric mixer, cream 2 tablespoons soft butter with cream cheese until fluffy. Beat in ¼ cup sugar, 1 egg, 1 tablespoon flour and 1 teaspoon vanilla. In a separate bowl, with wire whisk, beat 2 eggs until foamy. Add ¾ cup sugar, beating until well~blended. Stir in ½ cup flour, baking powder and salt until combined. Blend in melted chocolate mixture, vanilla, chopped almonds and almond extract. Spread ½ of chocolate batter evenly in pan. Spread cream cheese mixture over top. Drop spoonfuls of remaining chocolate batter on top of cheese layer, swirling top layers gently with a knife to marbleize.

 Bake about 45 minutes, or until top is golden and toothpick inserted in center comes out clean.

 Cool in pan completely before cutting into bars. Store in refrigerator.

Makes 20 brownies

Milk Chocolate Brownies

A double dose of milk chocolate adds to the smooth flavor and chewy texture of these bars.

¾ cup flour
¼ teaspoon salt
¼ teaspoon baking soda
⅓ cup butter
¾ cup sugar
2 tablespoons milk or cream

2 cups milk chocolate chips
1 teaspoon vanilla
2 eggs
1 cup chopped walnuts
~ powdered sugar ~

Preheat oven to 325.° Butter a 9" square pan.

In a small bowl, combine flour, salt and baking soda; set aside. In a small saucepan, melt butter, sugar and milk or cream together over low heat, stirring constantly. Bring mixture just to boiling, then remove from heat and imme~ diately stir in 1 cup of the chocolate chips and vanilla. Stir until chips melt and mixture is smooth. Transfer to a large bowl. Beat in eggs, one at a time. Blend in flour mixture. Fold in remaining 1 cup of chocolate chips and nuts. Spread batter evenly in pan.

Bake 30~35 minutes, or until toothpick inserted in center comes out clean. Cool in pan.

Dust top with powdered sugar and cut into squares.

Makes 25 brownies.

Chocolate Cherry Cordial Brownies

Real elegance ~ rich chocolate squares tinged with cherry liqueur and filled with crunchy almonds, chocolate bits and sweet cherries.

⅓ cup butter, softened
¾ cup brown sugar, packed
2 eggs
¼ cup light corn syrup
2 tablespoons Kirsch (cherry liqueur)
1 teaspoon vanilla
⅔ cup flour

⅓ cup unsweetened cocoa
½ teaspoon salt
¼ teaspoon baking powder
½ cup maraschino cherries, drained and quartered
⅓ cup each chopped almonds and chocolate chips

~ powdered sugar ~

Preheat oven to 350°. Butter a 9" square pan.

In a medium ~ sized bowl, cream together butter, sugar and eggs until thick and smooth. Blend in corn syrup, cherry liqueur and vanilla. In a small bowl, stir together flour, cocoa, salt and baking powder. Slowly add flour mixture to creamed mixture, blending well. Stir in cherries, almonds and chocolate chips. Combine thoroughly. Spread evenly in pan.

Bake 25~30 minutes, or until brownies begin to pull away from edges of pan. Cool completely on wire rack.

Sift powdered sugar over top and cut into squares.

Makes 16 brownies.

Optional garnish: sliced almonds pressed onto top before baking.

49

German Chocolate Brownies

Extra fudgy! Topped with a rich coconut~pecan~ chocolate chip frosting. Delicious cold.

2½ oz. unsweetened chocolate
½ cup butter, softened
¾ cup plus 2 tablespoons brown sugar, packed
2 eggs
¾ teaspoon vanilla
½ cup flour
Coconut Pecan Topping (recipe follows)

- Preheat oven to 350.° Butter an 8" square pan.

- Melt chocolate; set aside to cool. Cream butter with sugar and eggs. Stir in vanilla, then flour. Thoroughly blend in melted chocolate. Spread batter in pan.

- Bake about 20 minutes.

- Let cool in pan, then spread with Coconut Pecan Topping. Cut into squares.
Makes 16 brownies.

Coconut Pecan Topping

½ cup evaporated milk
½ cup sugar
2 egg yolks, slightly beaten
¼ cup butter
½ teaspoon vanilla
⅔ cup coconut, flaked or shredded
½ cup chopped pecans
¼ cup chocolate chips

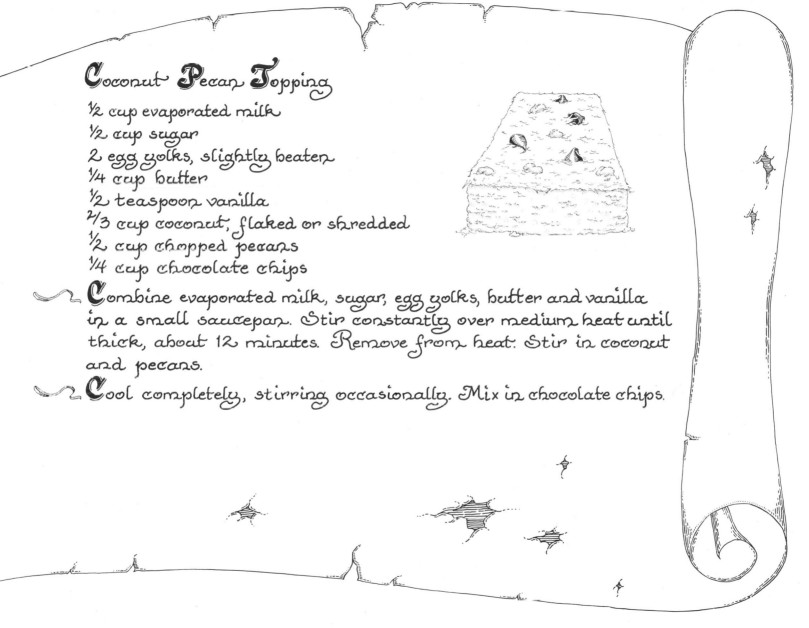

Combine evaporated milk, sugar, egg yolks, butter and vanilla in a small saucepan. Stir constantly over medium heat until thick, about 12 minutes. Remove from heat. Stir in coconut and pecans.

Cool completely, stirring occasionally. Mix in chocolate chips.

Pistachio Chocolate Swirl Brownies

Creamy chocolate and chewy pistachios together in a moist, satisfying brownie.

2 oz. unsweetened chocolate
1 cup butter, softened
2 cups sugar
1½ teaspoons vanilla
4 eggs
1¾ cups flour

½ teaspoon salt
½ teaspoon almond extract
1 cup chopped, shelled pistachios
green food coloring
1 cup chocolate chips

Preheat oven to 350°. Butter a 13 x 9 x 2" pan.

Melt chocolate; set aside to cool. In a large bowl, beat together butter, sugar and vanilla until light and fluffy. Beat in eggs, one at a time. Blend in flour and salt. Divide batter in half. To one half, add almond extract, chopped pistachios and enough food coloring to tint batter a pale green (2 ~ 4 drops). To remaining batter, stir in melted chocolate and chocolate chips; mix well. Spoon batters alternately into pan, checkerboard fashion. Swirl batters together with a knife to produce a marbled effect.

Bake about 45 minutes, or until toothpick inserted in center comes out clean.

Cool completely before cutting into bars.

Makes 32 brownies.

Cinnamon Fudge Brownies

Fudgy, cinnamon~scented squares.

¼ cup butter
2 oz. unsweetened chocolate
2 eggs
1 cup dark brown sugar, packed
¼ teaspoon salt
½ teaspoon vanilla
½ cup flour
1 teaspoon ground cinnamon
½ cup chopped pecans

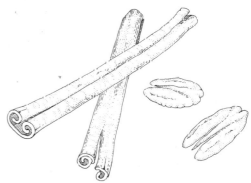

Preheat oven to 350.° Lightly butter an 8" square pan.

Melt chocolate and butter together over very low heat; set aside. In a medium~sized bowl, beat eggs with wire whisk; beat until light. Beat in sugar, salt and vanilla. Stir in melted chocolate mixture, then flour and cinnamon. Fold in pecans. Pour into pan.

Bake about 25 minutes, or until toothpick inserted in center comes out clean.

Cool completely in pan on wire rack before cutting into squares.

Makes 16 brownies.

∽ Capuccino Chip Brownies ∽

A creamy coffee~chocolate sensation.

2 cups vanilla wafer crumbs, lightly packed
1 14~oz. can sweetened condensed milk
1 rounded teaspoon instant coffee powder dissolved in a few drops boiling
    water
2 tablespoons unsweetened cocoa
½ cup chopped chocolate chips

∽ powdered sugar ∽

Preheat oven to 350°. Butter an 8" square pan.

In a medium~sized bowl, thoroughly stir together vanilla wafer crumbs and sweetened condensed milk. Blend in dissolved coffee powder and cocoa. Stir in chocolate chips. Spread batter evenly in pan.

Bake 25 minutes, or until done. Cool completely.

Sift powdered sugar lightly over top and cut into squares.
                   Makes 16 brownies.

LUSCIOUS NO~BAKE BROWNIES

These no~bake beauties have many advantages: they're relatively quick to put together, they last forever (well, almost) in a good hiding spot, they keep your kitchen cool by eliminating the use of your oven, and they are tremendously rich and delicious. Any disadvantages? You'll need a can of sweetened condensed milk and some cookie crumbs — no flour is used here. And there's some cooling time involved. But the real drawback is the tendency to overdo on their consumption. So beware, you have been forewarned!

Double Rocky Road Brownies

Almost a candy. Crunchy, dark and oh so fudgy!

2 cups semi~sweet chocolate chips
¼ cup butter
2 ½ cups vanilla wafer crumbs, lightly packed
1 14 oz. can sweetened condensed milk
2 cups miniature marshmallows
1 cup chopped walnuts or pecans
1 cup milk chocolate chips

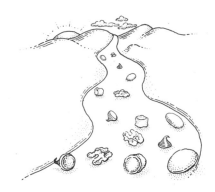

Lightly butter a 13 x 9 x 2" pan.

Melt semi~sweet chocolate chips and butter together over very low heat, stirring until smooth. In a large bowl, combine crumbs and sweetened condensed milk; mix well. Stir in melted chocolate mixture until well combined. Add marshmallows, nuts and milk chocolate chips using hands to mix, if necessary. Pat mixture into pan. Press paper towels firmly over surface of brownie, just to absorb excess moisture, then remove.

Let stand at room temperature for about 2 hours, then chill until firm. May be served chilled (for candy~like brownies) or at room temperature (for fudgier brownies). Cut into bars with a sharp knife.

Makes 48 brownies.

Butter Rum Raisin Brownies

A very sweet and spirited bar. A goody for the holidays.

1¾ cups dark or golden raisins, plumped *
¼ cup rum
¼ cup butter
2½ cups vanilla wafer crumbs, packed
1 14-oz. can sweetened condensed milk
¾ teaspoon rum extract
1 cup chopped walnuts
1 cup lightly toasted coconut

~powdered sugar~

* To plump raisins, pour boiling water over raisins, just to cover. Let stand 5~10 minutes, or until softened. Drain well. While still hot, mix with rum as directed above.

- **A**t least 2 hours before serving, soak hot plumped raisins in ¼ cup rum.
- **B**utter an 8" square pan.
- **M**elt butter over low heat. In a large bowl, combine vanilla wafer crumbs, butter, sweetened condensed milk and rum extract; mix well. Stir in nuts, coconut and raisin mixture. Combine well with a wooden spoon, or hands if necessary.
- **P**ress mixture evenly into pan. Chill until firm.
- **S**ift powdered sugar generously over top, then cut into small bars.

Makes 20 brownies.

Divinity Fudge Brownies

For a perfect holiday sweet, just add some red and green candied cherries.

12 oz. (¾ lb.) white chocolate (sold in stars or block form)
¼ cup butter
2 cups miniature marshmallows
2½ cups vanilla wafer crumbs, packed
1½ cups diced walnuts
1 14 oz. can sweetened condensed milk
1 teaspoon vanilla

~ 36 walnut halves or pieces ~

Lightly butter a 9" square pan.

In top of a double boiler over hot water, melt together chocolate and butter, stirring occasionally until smooth. Remove from hot water and gently fold in marshmallows. Do not overmix. In a large bowl, combine crumbs and diced walnuts; stir in sweetened condensed milk and vanilla until crumbs are thoroughly moistened. Gently stir in chocolate~marshmallow mixture, leaving batter lightly marbled. Pat mixture into pan. Lightly mark off squares with a knife, then press a walnut half into center of each square.

Let stand at room temperature about 2 hours, then chill briefly until firm. Cut into small squares. Serve at room temperature.

Makes 36 brownies.

Double Chocolate Malted Brownies

A soda fountain special in brownie form.

2 cups milk chocolate chips
¼ cup butter
2 cups vanilla wafer crumbs, lightly packed
½ cup instant malted milk powder, packed (natural flavor)
1 14 oz. can sweetened condensed milk
1 teaspoon vanilla
1½ cups chopped chocolate~covered malted milk balls

- Lightly butter a 9" square pan.
- Melt chocolate chips and butter together in top of a double boiler over hot water, stirring occasionally until smooth. In a large bowl, combine crumbs and malted milk powder. Thoroughly blend in sweetened condensed milk. Mix in vanilla and melted chocolate mixture. Fold in chopped malted milk balls. Spread batter evenly in pan. Press paper towels over top of brownie to absorb excess moisture; remove.
- Let brownie stand about 2 hours at room temperature, then chill until firm. Cut into squares. Serve cold or at room temperature.

Makes 25 brownies

Heavenly Ambrosia Brownies

Rich and sweet golden bars filled with tropical delights.

2½ cups vanilla wafer crumbs, lightly packed
¼ cup butter, melted
1 14-oz. can sweetened condensed milk
1 teaspoon vanilla
2 teaspoons finely grated fresh orange rind
2 cups miniature marshmallows
1 cup diced dried pineapple
⅔ cup chopped, lightly toasted almonds, cashews or macadamia nuts
⅔ cup lightly toasted flaked coconut

~ powdered sugar ~

Lightly butter a 9" square pan; set aside.

In a large bowl, combine crumbs, butter, sweetened condensed milk, vanilla and orange rind; mix well. Add marshmallows, pineapple, nuts and coconut. Use hands to combine thoroughly. Press mixture firmly into pan.

Let stand at room temperature about 1 hour.

Sift powdered sugar generously over top and chill until firm. Cut into bars with a sharp knife. May be served cold or at room temperature.
Makes 30 brownies.

Other possibilities: Banana chips; dried apricots or dates; candied or maraschino cherries.

Black Bottom Brownies

Luscious, no-bake, two-toned squares.

½ cup milk chocolate chips
½ cup semi-sweet chocolate chips
2 tablespoons butter
1¼ cups vanilla wafer crumbs, lightly packed
½ teaspoon vanilla

1 14-oz. can sweetened condensed milk
1¼ cups vanilla wafer crumbs, lightly packed
2 tablespoons butter, melted
½ teaspoon rum extract

Lightly butter an 8" square pan.

Over very low heat, melt together milk chocolate chips and semi-sweet chocolate chips with 2 tablespoons butter, stirring until smooth. Place 1¼ cups vanilla wafer crumbs in a small bowl. Stir in ½ can of sweetened condensed milk until crumbs are moistened. Thoroughly stir in melted chocolate mixture and ½ teaspoon vanilla. Pat mixture evenly in pan.

In another small bowl, stir remaining sweetened condensed milk into remaining 1¼ cups vanilla wafer crumbs. Mix in melted butter and rum extract. Spread carefully over chocolate layer in pan, patting batter to make an even layer.

Let stand at room temperature to harden, then chill briefly until firm. Cut into squares.

Makes 16 brownies.

～ White Chocolate Almond Brownies ～

Tastes like creamy almond bark fresh from a candy shop.

12 oz. (¾ lb.) white chocolate (sold in stars or block form)
2½ cups vanilla wafer crumbs, packed
1 14-oz. can sweetened condensed milk
1 teaspoon vanilla
1½ cups chopped, toasted almonds
～½ cup sliced, toasted almonds ～ (for topping)

Lightly butter a 9" square pan.

Melt chocolate in top of a double boiler over hot water; set aside. In a large bowl, combine vanilla wafer crumbs, sweetened condensed milk, vanilla and chopped almonds. Stir gently until all ingredients are moistened. Blend in melted chocolate until evenly mixed. Pat mix~ ture into pan. Sprinkle top with sliced almonds, pressing down lightly.

Let stand about 2 hours, then chill briefly until firm. Serve cold or at room temperature. Cut into small squares.

Makes 36 brownies

S'More Brownies

Like the real thing... only you don't have to camp out!

1 cup semi~sweet chocolate chips
¼ cup butter
2½ cups graham cracker crumbs
2 cups miniature marshmallows
1 14~oz. can sweetened condensed milk
1 teaspoon vanilla
1 cup milk chocolate chips

Lightly butter a 13x9x2" pan.

In a small saucepan, over very low heat, melt together butter and semi~sweet chocolate chips until smooth, stirring often. In a large bowl, combine graham cracker crumbs with marshmallows; stir in sweet~ened condensed milk and vanilla until crumbs are thoroughly moistened. Stir in melted chocolate mixture until well combined. Fold in milk chocolate chips. Pat into pan.

Let stand at room temperature about 2 hours before cutting. Chill, if a firmer brownie is desired.

Makes 32 brownies.

CHOCOLATE~CHIPPED BROWNIES

This is a section appealing to those who love anything and everything to do with chocolate chips. (Maybe you've even considered adopting one.) You'll find all kinds of batters here: peanut butter, coffee, brown sugar, coconut. All with one thing in common—lots and lots of rich, gooey chocolate chips. These brownies may make the humdrum chocolate chip cookie obsolete.

Note: You'll find a recipe for English Toffee Brownies in this section. Though there aren't any chocolate chips inside, there is a melted-on chocolate chip topping.

Orange Almond Crunch Brownies

Tangy orange, toasted almonds, dark chocolate. Need I say more?

2 cups vanilla wafer crumbs, lightly packed
1 14~oz. can sweetened condensed milk
1 teaspoon orange extract
1 heaping teaspoon freshly grated orange rind
1 cup chopped toasted almonds
½ cup chopped chocolate chips

Preheat oven to 350°. Butter an 8" square pan.

In a medium~sized bowl, thoroughly stir together vanilla wafer crumbs and sweetened condensed milk. Blend in orange extract and rind. Fold in almonds and chocolate chips. Spread batter evenly in pan.

Bake about 25 minutes, or until brownies test done.

Let cool completely in pan before cutting into squares.

Makes 16 brownies.

Crunchy Vanilla Pecan Brownies

Nutty chocolate~flecked vanilla squares.

2 cups vanilla wafer crumbs, lightly packed
1 14~oz. can sweetened condensed milk
2 teaspoons vanilla
1 cup finely chopped toasted pecans
½ cup chopped milk chocolate chips

~powdered sugar~

Preheat oven to 350°. Butter an 8" square pan.

In a medium~sized bowl, blend together vanilla wafer crumbs and sweetened condensed milk. Stir in vanilla, then pecans and chocolate chips. Spread batter firmly in pan.

Bake 25~30 minutes, or until toothpick inserted in center comes out clean. Cool completely.

Sift powdered sugar over top and cut into squares.

Makes 16 brownies.

English Toffee Brownies

Candy disguised as a brownie.

1 cup butter, softened
1 cup dark brown sugar, packed
1 egg yolk
1 ½ teaspoons vanilla
2 cups sifted flour (sift before measuring)
1 cup chocolate chips
2 tablespoons _each_ butter and water
1 cup very finely chopped walnuts

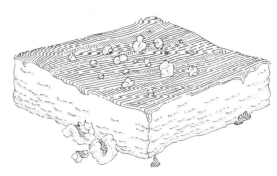

Preheat oven to 350°. Lightly butter a 13 x 9 x 2" pan.

In a large bowl, using electric mixer, beat together 1 cup butter and sugar until light and fluffy. Beat in egg yolk and vanilla. Stir in flour until well blended. Pat mixture into pan, using wet hands, if necessary, to make an even layer.

Bake about 25 minutes, or until golden.

Meanwhile, combine chocolate chips, 2 tablespoons butter and water in top of a double boiler. Melt over simmering water, stirring until smooth. Spread chocolate mixture over hot baked layer and immediately sprinkle with nuts. Cool 15 minutes, then cut into bars.

Cool completely, then chill briefly to harden.

Makes 32 brownies

∽ Oatmeal Date Nut Brownies ∽

A good snack bar. Excellent with a cold glass of milk.

2 cups flour
1 teaspoon baking soda
1 teaspoon salt
1 cup butter, softened
1½ cups brown sugar, packed
2 eggs
1 tablespoon orange juice

1 rounded teaspoon grated orange rind
1½ cups rolled oats
1 cup chopped dates
1 cup chopped walnuts
½ cup chopped chocolate chips
∽ powdered sugar ∽

Preheat oven to 375.° Butter a 13 x 9 x 2" pan.

In a small bowl, combine flour, baking soda and salt; set aside. In a large bowl, using an electric mixer, beat butter, sugar, eggs, orange juice and orange rind until creamy. Gradually blend in flour mixture. Stir in oats, dates, nuts and chocolate chips. Spread batter evenly in pan.

Bake 25 minutes, or until golden and toothpick inserted in center comes out clean. Cool completely in pan.

Sift powdered sugar over top, and cut into bars.

Makes 32 brownies.

Cherry Bonbon Brownies

Snow~topped cherry~chocolate confections.

2¼ cups vanilla wafer crumbs, lightly packed
1 14~oz. can sweetened condensed milk
¼ cup cherry preserves
1 teaspoon vanilla
½ cup cut up candied red cherries
½ cup chopped chocolate chips

~powdered sugar~
10 candied red cherries, halved

Preheat oven to 350.° Butter an 8" square pan.

In a medium~sized bowl, combine vanilla wafer crumbs and sweetened condensed milk; mix well. Blend in cherry preserves and vanilla. Fold in ½ cup candied cherries and chocolate chips. Spread batter evenly in pan.

Bake 25~30 minutes, or until brownies are done. Cool thoroughly in pan.

Sift powdered sugar over top and cut into squares. Place a candied cherry half in the center of each brownie.

Makes 16 brownies.

Coconut Macaroon Chip Brownies

Chewy squares filled with sweet coconut, ground almonds and chocolate bits.

2 egg whites, room temperature
1 cup powdered sugar (sift after measuring)
1 cup ground, blanched almonds
1⅓ cups coconut
1½ teaspoons almond liqueur
⅓ cup chopped chocolate chips

~ powdered sugar ~

Preheat oven to 300°. Butter an 8" square pan.

In a medium ~ sized bowl with electric mixer, beat egg whites until stiff but not dry. Fold in ½ cup of the powdered sugar and ground almonds. Stir in coco~ nut, remaining powdered sugar, liqueur and chocolate chips. With a rubber spatula, work into a sticky dough. Spread in pan.

Bake 25 ~ 30 minutes, or until firm and lightly golden around edges. Cool com~ pletely in pan on wire rack.

Sift powdered sugar over top and chill. Cut into squares with a sharp knife and serve cold.

Makes 16 brownies.

Chewy Coffee Chip Brownies

Coffee and chocolate. Is there a better combination?

2 cups vanilla wafer crumbs, lightly packed
1 14 oz. can sweetened condensed milk
1 rounded teaspoon instant coffee powder, dissolved in a few drops boiling water to dilute
½ cup chopped milk chocolate chips
½ cup chopped almonds, lightly toasted

- Preheat oven to 350°. Butter an 8" square pan.
- In a medium~sized bowl, combine crumbs, sweetened condensed milk and dissolved coffee powder; stir well to moisten thoroughly. Fold in chocolate chips and almonds. Spread batter evenly in pan.
- Bake 25~30 minutes, or until done.
- Cool completely in pan. Cut into squares.

Makes 16 brownies.

Maple Walnut Brownies

Quick to make. Quick to disappear!

2 cups vanilla wafer crumbs, lightly packed
1 can 14-oz. sweetened condensed milk
1 teaspoon maple extract
2/3 cup chopped walnuts
2/3 cup lightly toasted shredded coconut
2/3 cup milk chocolate chips

~ powdered sugar ~

Preheat oven to 350°. Lightly butter an 8" square pan.

In a medium-sized bowl, combine crumbs with sweetened condensed milk, moistening thoroughly. Stir in maple extract; then walnuts, coconut and chocolate chips. Combine well. Spread batter in pan.

Bake 25-30 minutes. Cool completely in pan.

Lightly sift powdered sugar over top and cut into squares.

Makes 16 brownies.

Fruity Spumoni Brownies

A myriad of colors and flavors in every chewy bite.

2 cups vanilla wafer crumbs, lightly packed
1 14-oz. can sweetened condensed milk
1 teaspoon rum extract
½ cup chopped, shelled pistachio nuts
½ cup currants
½ cup cut up red and green candied cherries
½ cup chopped milk chocolate chips

~ powdered sugar ~

Preheat oven to 350°. Butter a 9" square pan.

In a medium-sized bowl, combine vanilla wafer crumbs and sweetened condensed milk; mix well. Blend in rum extract. Gently fold in pistachios, currants, candied cherries and chocolate chips until uniformly distributed. Spread batter evenly in pan.

Bake about 30 minutes, or until golden and toothpick inserted in center comes out clean. Cool.

Sift powdered sugar generously over top and cut into bars.

Makes 20 brownies.

～ Burnt Almond Chip Brownies ～

Luscious brown sugar bars filled with toasted almonds, sweet chocolate bits, and just a hint of Amaretto.

½ cup butter
2 cups brown sugar, packed
2 eggs
1 teaspoon vanilla
¼ cup Amaretto liqueur
2 cups flour
¼ cup lightly toasted ground
   blanched almonds, packed

2 teaspoons baking powder
¼ teaspoon salt
1½ cups finely chopped roasted
   almonds (unblanched)
½ cup chopped chocolate chips
～ powdered sugar ～

Preheat oven to 350°. Butter a 13x9x2" pan.

In a large saucepan, melt butter. Remove from heat and blend in brown sugar. Beat in eggs and vanilla. Stir in Amaretto, flour, ground almonds, baking powder and salt; mix well. Fold in chopped almonds and chocolate chips. Spread batter in pan.

Bake about 25 minutes, or until golden and toothpick inserted in center comes out clean. Cool in pan.

Sift powdered sugar over top and cut into bars.
Makes 32 brownies.

Peanut Butter Cup Brownies

Try these with an icy cold glass of milk.

1 cup flour
1 teaspoon baking powder
¼ teaspoon salt
½ cup peanut butter
⅓ cup butter, softened
1 cup brown sugar, packed
2 eggs
1 teaspoon vanilla
1 cup chocolate chips

Preheat oven to 350°. Butter a 9" square pan.

In a small bowl, stir together flour, baking powder and salt; set aside. In a medium~sized bowl, beat together peanut butter, butter and sugar until fluffy. Beat in eggs, one by one. Blend in vanilla. Gradually stir in flour mixture just until combined. Fold in chocolate chips. Spread batter evenly in pan.

Bake 25~30 minutes, or until toothpick inserted in center comes out clean.

Cool completely before cutting into bars.

Makes 20 brownies.

Cinnamon Honey Graham Cracker Brownies

With a cup of hot cocoa, perhaps.

2 cups graham cracker crumbs
1 teaspoon cinnamon
1 14~oz. can sweetened condensed milk
¼ cup honey
¾ cup plain or cinnamon granola
¾ cup chocolate chips

 Preheat oven to 350° Butter a 9" square pan.

 In a medium~sized bowl, combine graham cracker crumbs and cinnamon. Thoroughly blend in sweetened condensed milk and honey. Fold in granola and chocolate chips. Spread batter evenly in pan.

 Bake 30~35 minutes, or until toothpick inserted in center comes out clean.

 Cool completely before cutting into bars.

Makes 20 brownies.

Honeycomb Chip Brownies

A deliciously thick and moist brownie—rich with honey, brown sugar and a touch of chocolate.

½ cup butter
¾ cup brown sugar
¼ cup honey
2 eggs
1 teaspoon vanilla
¼ teaspoon salt
1 cup flour
½ cup chopped chocolate chips

Preheat oven to 350.° Butter an 8" square pan.

In a small saucepan, melt butter over low heat. Remove from heat and beat in brown sugar and honey; cool slightly. In a medium-sized bowl, beat eggs well. Gradually beat in butter~sugar mixture. Blend in vanilla and salt. Thoroughly mix in flour. Fold in chocolate chips. Pour batter into pan.

Bake 20~25 minutes, or until toothpick inserted in center comes out clean.

Cool completely in pan. Cut into squares.

Makes 16 brownies.

CHOCOLATE~LESS BROWNIES

Brownies without chocolate? Oh, you're probably familiar with butterscotch or peanut butter, but how about Toasted Cashew, Chinese Almond, or Carrot Coconut Brownies for starters? Then of course there's Golden Eggnog and Spiced Apple. You get the idea. Bake a batch and see for yourself just how irresistible brownies can be— even without the chocolate.

Peanut Butter and Banana Brownies

Soft and cake. Bursting with creamy peanut butter chips.

1 cup flour
1 teaspoon baking powder
¼ teaspoon salt
⅓ cup butter, softened
½ cup peanut butter
½ cup granulated sugar
½ cup brown sugar, packed
2 eggs
1 teaspoon vanilla
½ cup mashed, very ripe banana
1 cup peanut butter chips

~ powdered sugar ~

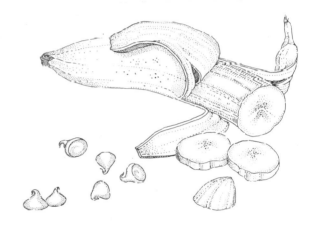

Preheat oven to 350.° Butter a 9" square pan.

In a small bowl, stir together flour, baking powder and salt. In a large bowl, using a wire whisk, cream together butter, peanut butter and sugars until fluffy. Beat in eggs, vanilla and mashed banana until creamy. Stir in flour mixture just to combine. Fold in peanut butter chips. Spread batter in pan.

Bake 30~35 minutes, or until toothpick inserted in center comes out clean.

Cool completely. Sift powdered sugar over top, and cut into bars.

Makes 20 brownies.

Carrot Coconut Brownies

Carrot cake in a chewy, moist bar.

1 cup flour
½ teaspoon salt
½ teaspoon baking powder
⅛ teaspoon baking soda
½ teaspoon each cinnamon and nutmeg
⅓ cup butter
1 cup brown sugar, packed
1 egg
1 teaspoon vanilla
⅓ cup finely grated carrot, packed
⅓ cup diced dried pineapple
¼ cup coconut
¼ cup raisins or currants
¼ cup diced walnuts

Orange Cream Cheese Frosting (recipe follows)
~24 walnut halves~

Preheat oven to 350°. Butter a 9" square pan.

In a small bowl, combine flour, salt, baking powder, baking soda and spices; set aside. In a medium-sized saucepan, melt butter over low heat. Remove from heat and beat in sugar, then egg and vanilla. Stir in carrots and flour mixture thoroughly. Fold in pineapple, coconut, raisins and walnuts. Combine gently. Pour into pan.

~ Bake 30 minutes, or until golden and toothpick inserted in center comes out clean. Let cool completely in pan.

~ Frost with Orange Cream Cheese Frosting and let set until firm.

~ Mark into bars and press a walnut half into center of each bar. Chill, then cut through bars with a sharp knife.

Makes 24 brownies.

Orange Cream Cheese Frosting

1½ oz. cream cheese, softened
1½ teaspoons orange juice (fresh is best)
½ teaspoon vanilla
1¼ cups powdered sugar
dash of freshly grated orange rind

~ Blend cream cheese with orange juice and vanilla. Gradually add powdered sugar, beating until creamy. Blend in orange rind.

Note: Carrot cake lovers better double up on this one. Use a 13x9x2" pan.

Gingerbread Graham Cracker Brownies

Spicy and delicious. They last forever in the refrigerator ~ if you can hide them!

2 cups graham cracker crumbs
1½ teaspoons ginger
½ teaspoon nutmeg
¼ teaspoon allspice
1 14 oz. can sweetened condensed milk
¼ cup dark molasses
2/3 cup butterscotch chips
2/3 cup currants or raisins
2/3 cup diced walnuts

~ powdered sugar ~

Preheat oven to 350°. Butter an 8" square pan.

In a large bowl, combine crumbs with spices. Thoroughly stir in sweetened condensed milk and molasses. Add butterscotch chips, dried fruit and nuts; mix well. Spread evenly in pan.

Bake 30~35 minutes. Cool completely in pan.

Sift powdered sugar generously over top, and cut into bars.

Makes 24 brownies.

～ Coconut Key Lime Brownies ～

Easier than pie to make and to eat.

2 ¼ cups vanilla wafer crumbs, lightly packed
1 14~oz. can sweetened condensed milk
¼ cup fresh lime juice
1 tablespoon grated lime peel
1 cup shredded coconut

～ powdered sugar ～

- **P**reheat oven to 350.° Butter an 8" square pan.
- **I**n a medium~sized bowl, thoroughly blend together vanilla wafer crumbs and sweetened condensed milk. Stir in lime juice and peel. Mix in coconut. Spread batter evenly in pan.
- **B**ake about 25 minutes, or until toothpick inserted in center comes out clean. Cool in pan.
- **S**ift powdered sugar generously over top before cutting.

Makes 16 brownies.

For an **E**xotic **C**runch, sprinkle some chopped macadamia nuts on top just before baking.

⊷ Pumpkin Praline Brownies ⊷

Better than pumpkin pie!

2 eggs, beaten
½ cup butter, melted
1 cup brown sugar, packed
¼ cup honey
1 cup pumpkin puree
2 cups flour
1 teaspoon cinnamon
½ teaspoon _each_ salt, baking soda and ginger
¼ teaspoon _each_ cloves and allspice
1 cup chopped pecans
¾ cup butterscotch chips
Creamy Cream Cheese Frosting (recipe follows)
⊷ 32 pecan halves ⊷

Preheat oven to 350.° Butter a 13 x 9 x 2" pan.

Cream together eggs, butter, sugar, honey and pumpkin. In a separate bowl, stir together flour, cinnamon, salt, baking soda, ginger, cloves and allspice. Slowly add dry ingredients to creamed mixture, stir~ring just to combine. Fold in chopped pecans and butterscotch chips. Pour batter into pan.

84

🎃 **B**ake about 25 minutes, or until toothpick inserted in center comes out clean. Cool completely in pan on wire rack.

🎃 **S**pread with Creamy Cream Cheese Frosting, then let set to harden.

🎃 **M**ark into bars and press a pecan half in center of each brownie. Chill, then cut through into bars.

Makes 32 brownies.

Creamy Cream Cheese Frosting

1 3-oz. package cream cheese, softened
1 tablespoon cream or milk
1 teaspoon vanilla
2 ½ cups powdered sugar

🎃 **C**ream together cheese, cream (or milk) and vanilla. Gradually add sugar, beating until smooth. Add more cream or milk, if necessary, to achieve a spreading consistency.

Chinese Almond Brownies

Chinese fortune cookie says, "You are in for a scrumptious treat!"

2 cups vanilla wafer crumbs, lightly packed
1 cup ground, blanched raw almonds
1 14~oz. can sweetened condensed milk
1 teaspoon almond extract
1 egg yolk, beaten with 1½ teaspoons water
~ 20 whole blanched almonds ~

 Preheat oven to 350°. Lightly butter a 9" square pan.

 In a medium~sized bowl, stir together vanilla wafer crumbs and ground almonds. Work in sweetened condensed milk and almond extract until all is moistened. Spread batter evenly in pan. Brush surface with some of egg yolk mixture. Press whole blanched almonds onto top, making 4 by 5 rows, spacing evenly. Brush entire surface with more egg yolk mixture.

Bake brownies about 25 minutes, or until done. Cool completely in pan.

Cut through brownies, leaving a whole blanched almond in center of each. Remove bars carefully with a spatula.
Makes 20 brownies.

Lemony Tutti-Frutti Brownies

Chewy and fruity.

2 cups vanilla wafer crumbs, lightly packed
1 14-oz. can sweetened condensed milk
1 teaspoon lemon extract
1 teaspoon freshly grated lemon or orange peel
½ cup diced dried figs
½ cup chopped golden raisins
½ cup shredded coconut
½ cup finely chopped walnuts
~ powdered sugar ~

Preheat oven to 350°. Butter a 9" square pan.

In a medium-sized bowl, stir sweetened condensed milk into vanilla wafer crumbs; mix well. Blend in extract and lemon or orange peel. Work in figs, raisins, coconut and walnuts. Spread batter evenly in pan.

Bake about 25 minutes, or until toothpick inserted in center comes out clean. Cool.

Sift powdered sugar over top and cut into bars.

Makes 20 brownies.

◌ Chunky Mincemeat Brownies ◌

For extra moistness and flavor, age a day before serving. Nice for drop~in guests at holiday time!

2 cups flour
½ teaspoon <u>each</u> baking powder, baking soda and cinnamon
½ cup butter, softened
⅓ cup sugar
⅓ cup dark molasses
1 egg
2 tablespoons brandy
1 cup mincemeat
¾ cup finely chopped walnuts
¾ cup currants

Brandy Butter Icing (recipe follows)
◌ 32 walnut halves ◌

Preheat oven to 350.° Butter a 13 x 9 x 2" pan.

In a small bowl, stir together flour, baking powder, baking soda and cinnamon; set aside. In a large bowl with electric mixer, beat together butter, sugar, molasses and egg until light and fluffy. Blend in brandy and mincemeat. Gradually beat in flour mixture until well combined. Stir in walnuts and currants. Spread batter evenly in pan, making a smooth top.

⊛ Bake about 25 minutes, or until toothpick inserted in center comes out clean. Cool completely in pan.

⊛ Frost brownies with Brandy Butter Icing and let set until firm.

⊛ Cut carefully into bars. Press a walnut half into center of each. Chill, or serve at room temperature.

Makes 32 brownies.

Brandy Butter Icing

¼ cup butter, softened.
2 cups powdered sugar
brandy

⊛ Blend together butter and sugar. Stir in enough brandy, about 2 tablespoons, to achieve a spreadable consistency. Beat until creamy ~ smooth.

Crunchy Peanut Butter and Jelly Brownies

Moist peanut butter squares with toasty peanuts and swirls of your favorite jelly or jam. A wonderful lunch box treat for kids.

1 cup flour
1 teaspoon baking powder
¼ teaspoon salt
½ cup peanut butter
⅓ cup butter, softened
½ cup granulated sugar

½ cup brown sugar, packed
2 eggs
1 teaspoon vanilla
½ heaping cup chopped toasted peanuts
½ cup jelly or jam (your favorite)

Preheat oven to 350°. Lightly butter a 9" square pan.

In a small bowl, stir together flour, baking powder and salt; set aside. In a medium~sized bowl, using electric mixer, cream together peanut butter, butter and sugars until fluffy. Beat in eggs and vanilla until well blended. Stir in flour mixture just to combine. Fold in ½ of the chopped peanuts. Spread batter evenly in pan. With a spoon, drop dollops of jelly checkerboard fashion onto peanut butter layer. Run a knife through batter to produce a marbled effect. With a wet hand, gently smooth top of batter to make even. Sprinkle with remaining peanuts.

Bake 30~35 minutes, or until slight imprint remains when top is lightly pressed in center.

Cool thoroughly in pan on wire rack. Cut into bars.

Makes 20 brownies

Chewy Butterscotch Brownies

Crunchy with peanuts.... chewy with coconut.

¼ cup butter
1 cup brown sugar, packed
1 egg
½ teaspoon vanilla
1 cup flour
1 teaspoon baking powder
⅛ teaspoon salt
½ cup shredded coconut, lightly toasted
½ cup chopped peanuts

~ powdered sugar ~

Preheat oven to 350°. Butter a 9" square pan.

In a small saucepan, melt butter. Remove from heat and blend in brown sugar. Beat in egg and vanilla. In a small bowl, combine flour, baking powder and salt. Stir dry ingredients into creamed mixture, blending well. Fold in coconut and pea~nuts. Spread evenly in pan.

Bake about 25 minutes or until done. Cut into bars while still warm.

Dust with powdered sugar before serving.

Makes 20 brownies.

Turkish Apricot Crème Brownies

Moist and luscious, with swirls of apricot cream.

¼ cup butter, softened
2 3~oz. packages cream cheese, softened
½ cup sugar
2 eggs
2 tablespoons flour
2 teaspoons vanilla (or 1 teaspoon vanilla and ½ teaspoon almond extract)
2 cups diced dried Turkish apricots

⅔ cup butter
2 cups brown sugar, packed
2 eggs
2 teaspoons vanilla
2 cups flour
1 teaspoon baking powder
1 teaspoon salt
¼ teaspoon baking soda
1 cup lightly toasted shredded coconut

Preheat oven to 350°. Butter a 13 x 9 x 2" pan.

In a small bowl, beat together ¼ cup softened butter and cream cheese until fluffy. Add ½ cup sugar, 2 eggs, 2 tablespoons flour and 2 teaspoons vanilla; beat well. Fold in diced apricots; set aside.

In a large saucepan, melt ⅔ cup butter. Remove from heat, and stir in brown sugar. Beat in 2 eggs and 2 teaspoons vanilla. Stir in 2 cups flour, baking powder, salt and baking soda; blend well. Fold in coconut.

Spread ½ of coconut batter evenly in pan. Spread cream cheese mixture over top, covering batter completely. Spoon dollops of remaining coconut batter over cream cheese layer, covering as much as possible. Lightly swirl top batters with a knife.

Bake about 50 minutes, or until golden, and toothpick in~ serted in center comes out clean.

Cool completely in pan. Chill, then cut into bars.

Makes 40 brownies

93

Toasted Cashew Brownies

Ah! The aroma of freshly roasted cashews.

2 cups vanilla wafer crumbs, lightly packed
1 cup ground raw cashews
1 14-oz. can sweetened condensed milk
¼ cup honey
1 teaspoon vanilla
1 cup chopped, toasted cashews
½ cup shredded coconut

Preheat oven to 350°. Butter a 9" square pan.

In a medium-sized bowl, stir together vanilla wafer crumbs and ground cashews. Thoroughly blend in sweetened condensed milk and honey. Stir in vanilla, chopped toasted cashews and coconut; mix well. Turn batter into pan, spreading evenly.

Bake about 25 minutes, or until toothpick inserted in center comes out clean.

Cool completely before cutting.
Makes 20 brownies.

Lemon Poppyseed Brownies

Snow~capped, lemony squares. A perfect luncheon dessert.

2 cups vanilla wafer crumbs, lightly packed
1 14~oz. can sweetened condensed milk
1 teaspoon lemon extract
1 teaspoon freshly grated lemon peel
2 ~ 4 tablespoons poppyseeds (depending upon your liking)
2/3 cup finely chopped walnuts
2/3 cup currants

~ powdered sugar ~

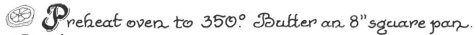

Preheat oven to 350°. Butter an 8" square pan.

In a medium~sized bowl, combine crumbs, sweetened condensed milk, lemon extract and lemon peel until ingredients are moistened. Stir in poppyseeds, walnuts and currants; mix well. Spread in pan.

Bake 25~30 minutes, or until done. Cool completely on wire rack.

Sift powdered sugar generously over top. Cut into squares.

Makes 16 brownies.

Spiced Apple Brownies

These lightly spiced, fruity bars age well under refrigeration.

1 cup flour
½ teaspoon salt
½ teaspoon baking powder
⅛ teaspoon baking soda
1 teaspoon cinnamon
½ teaspoon nutmeg
¼ teaspoon cloves
⅓ cup butter

1 cup brown sugar, packed
1 egg
1 teaspoon vanilla
⅓ cup grated pared tart apple, packed
½ cup finely chopped walnuts
½ cup raisins, currants or chopped dates
Vanilla Cream Icing (recipe follows)
24 walnut halves or chopped walnuts

Preheat oven to 350.° Butter a 9" square pan.

In a small bowl, stir together flour, salt, baking powder, baking soda and spices; set aside. In a medium-sized saucepan, melt butter. Remove from heat and stir in brown sugar. Beat in egg and vanilla. Gently stir in apple, then flour mixture. Fold in nuts and dried fruit. Spread batter evenly in pan.

Bake 25~30 minutes, or until toothpick inserted in center comes out clean. Do not overbake.

Cool completely in pan, then frost with Vanilla Cream Icing. Decorate with walnuts, then cut into bars. Delicious chilled. Makes 24 brownies.

Vanilla Cream Icing

2 tablespoons butter, softened
1 cup powdered sugar
½ teaspoon vanilla
about 1 tablespoon milk or cream

Blend together butter and sugar. Stir in vanilla and milk; beat until smooth and creamy. Add more milk, if icing is too thick to spread easily.

Caramel Coconut Pecan Brownies

Crunchy pecans, chewy coconut, creamy caramel. Yum!

2 cups vanilla wafer crumbs, packed
1 14~oz. can sweetened condensed milk
1 teaspoon vanilla
1 cup shredded coconut
1 cup coarsely chopped pecans

½ cup butter
⅓ cup brown sugar, packed

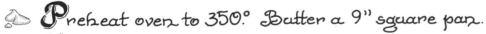 **P**reheat oven to 350°. Butter a 9" square pan.

In a small bowl, blend together vanilla wafer crumbs and sweetened con~ densed milk. Work in vanilla and coconut. Spread batter evenly in pan. Sprinkle top with pecans; set aside.

In a small saucepan, bring butter and brown sugar to a boil, stirring. Simmer 1 minute, stirring constantly. Carefully pour hot caramel mix~ ture over pecans, covering entire top.

Bake about 25 minutes, or until caramel is bubbling all over top of brownie.

Cool completely. Cut into bars with a sharp knife.

Makes 20 brownies.

Irish Coffee Brownies

A nutty coffee brownie with an Irish twist.

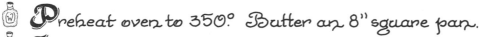

¼ cup whiskey
1 tablespoon instant coffee powder
2 ¼ cups vanilla wafer crumbs, lightly packed
1 14~oz. can sweetened condensed milk
1 cup broken walnuts

~ powdered sugar ~

Preheat oven to 350°. Butter an 8" square pan.

In a small saucepan over a very low flame, heat whiskey until hot. Stir in coffee powder to dissolve; set aside to cool. In a medium~sized bowl, thoroughly stir together vanilla wafer crumbs and sweetened condensed milk. Blend in whiskey~coffee mixture, then walnuts. Mix well. Spread batter evenly in pan.

Bake 25 minutes, or until toothpick inserted in center comes out clean. Cool on wire rack.

Sift powdered sugar over top and cut into squares.

Makes 16 brownies.

Peanut Brittle Cream Brownies

A triple peanut butter treat!

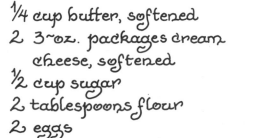

¼ cup butter, softened
2 3-oz. packages cream
  cheese, softened
½ cup sugar
2 tablespoons flour
2 eggs
2 teaspoons vanilla
1 cup chopped peanut brittle

1 cup peanut butter
½ cup butter, softened
2 cups light brown sugar, packed
3 eggs
1 teaspoon vanilla
1 cup flour
½ teaspoon salt
1 cup peanut butter chips

Preheat oven to 350.° Butter a 13 x 9 x 2" pan.

In a medium-sized bowl, beat together ¼ cup softened butter and cream cheese until fluffy. Add ½ cup sugar, 2 tablespoons flour, 2 eggs and 2 teaspoons vanilla; beat until creamy. Stir in peanut brittle; set aside.

In another bowl, beat together peanut butter and ½ cup softened butter. Add brown sugar, 3 eggs and 1 teaspoon vanilla; beat until light and fluffy. Blend in 1 cup flour and salt. Fold in peanut butter chips.

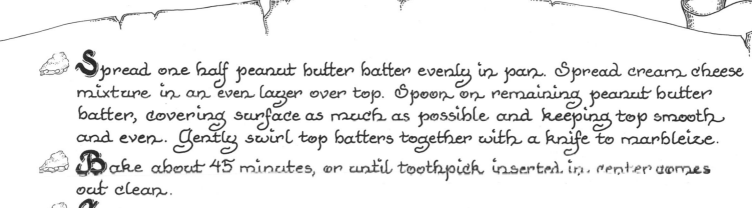 **S**pread one half peanut butter batter evenly in pan. Spread cream cheese mixture in an even layer over top. Spoon on remaining peanut butter batter, covering surface as much as possible and keeping top smooth and even. Gently swirl top batters together with a knife to marbleize.

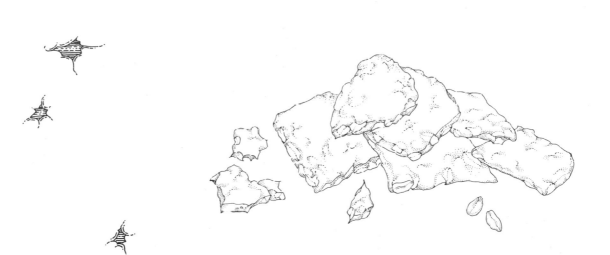 **B**ake about 45 minutes, or until toothpick inserted in center comes out clean.

Cool completely. Cut into bars. Best served chilled.

Makes 32 brownies.

Golden Eggnog Brownies

Old fashioned eggnog enjoyed in a brand new way.

2¼ cups vanilla wafer crumbs, lightly packed
1 teaspoon nutmeg
1 14~oz. can sweetened condensed milk
2 tablespoons golden rum
½ teaspoon rum extract
2 egg yolks, beaten
½ cup chopped golden raisins
½ cup finely diced walnuts

~ extra nutmeg ~
~ powdered sugar ~

Preheat oven to 350°. Butter an 8" square pan.

In a medium~sized bowl, stir together vanilla wafer crumbs and nutmeg. Thoroughly blend in sweetened condensed milk. Stir in rum, rum extract and beaten egg yolks; mix well. Fold in raisins and walnuts. Spread batter evenly in pan. Sprinkle top generously with extra nutmeg.

Bake 20~25 minutes, or until toothpick inserted in center comes out clean. Cool in pan.

Lightly sift powdered sugar over top and cut into squares.

Makes 16 brownies.

Chunky Black Walnut Brownies

If you like black walnut ice cream, you'll love these irresistibly chewy bars.

2 cups vanilla wafer crumbs, lightly packed
1 14-oz. can sweetened condensed milk
1 teaspoon black walnut extract
1 cup chopped black walnuts
½ cup cut up golden raisins

~powdered sugar~

CHUNKY BLACK WALNUT

Preheat oven to 350.° Butter an 8" square pan.

In a medium-sized bowl, combine vanilla wafer crumbs and sweetened condensed milk; mix well. Stir in extract, then walnuts and raisins. Spread batter evenly in pan.

Bake 25~30 minutes, or until firm. Do not overbake. Cool completely in pan.

Dust powdered sugar over top and cut into squares.

Makes 16 brownies.

Sesame Honey Brownies

Sesame seed lovers unite! These are incredible.

2 cups vanilla wafer crumbs, lightly packed
1 cup ground raw sesame seeds   (grind in blender)
1 14-oz. can sweetened condensed milk
¼ cup honey
1 cup lightly toasted sesame seeds

- Preheat oven to 350.° Butter a 9" square pan.
- In a medium-sized bowl, combine vanilla wafer crumbs and ground sesame seeds. Thoroughly blend in sweetened condensed milk and honey. Stir in toasted sesame seeds until evenly distributed. Spread batter into pan.
- Bake 25~30 minutes, or until toothpick inserted in center comes out clean.
- Cool. Cut into bars with a sharp knife.

Makes 20 brownies.

HEALTH CONSCIOUS BROWNIES

Here is a way to have your cake (or brownie) and eat it too! Almost everyone nowadays is concerned about what foods they put into their bodies. When we're lucky enough to discover treats that not only satisfy our sweet tooths, but also some of our nutritional needs, we feel extra good about eating them. They become part of a meal — not just added empty calories. What follows are some brownie recipes incorporating as many healthy goodies as possible: whole wheat, peanut butter, honey, carob, wheat germ, nuts, dried fruit and more. They're all deliciously healthy, and provide more protein, fiber, and sustaining food energy than the usual sweet snack. Here's to your good health!

Honey Fudge Brownies

Super~rich chocolate brownies made the natural way~with honey and whole wheat.

2 oz. unsweetened chocolate
¼ cup butter
2 eggs
¾ cup honey
½ teaspoon vanilla
¼ teaspoon salt
¾ cup whole wheat pastry flour
¾ cup chopped pecans

Preheat oven to 350°. Lightly butter an 8" square pan.

In a small saucepan, over low heat, melt together chocolate and butter; let cool. In a medium~sized bowl, beat eggs until light using a wire whisk. Gradually beat in honey, then vanilla and salt. Blend in melt~ed chocolate mixture. Thoroughly stir in flour and pecans. Pour batter into pan.

Bake about 20 minutes, or until toothpick inserted in center comes out clean.

Cool completely before cutting into squares.

Makes 16 brownies.

Banana Oatmeal Chip Brownies

Tastes like an all-natural banana bread brownie.

3/4 cup butter, softened
3/4 cup honey
1 egg
3/4 cup mashed, ripe banana
1½ cups whole wheat pastry flour
½ teaspoon each baking soda, salt and nutmeg
1½ cups raw rolled oats
1 cup carob chips
1 cup finely chopped walnuts or pecans

Preheat oven to 375.° Butter a 13 x 9 x 2" pan.

In a large bowl, beat together butter, honey and egg until creamy. Beat in mashed banana. In a small bowl, stir together flour, baking soda, salt and nutmeg. Gradually beat dry ingredients into creamed mixture. Stir in oats, carob chips and walnuts; mix well. Spread batter evenly in pan.

Bake 20~25 minutes, or until toothpick inserted in center comes out clean.

Cool completely. Chill to make cutting easier. Cut into bars and care~ fully remove from pan.

Makes 32 brownies.

Peanut Butter and Carob Fudge Brownies

Dark, rich brownie confections so good you won't believe they're healthy.

¼ cup peanut butter
¼ cup butter
2 eggs
¾ cup honey
1 teaspoon vanilla

¼ teaspoon salt
½ cup whole wheat pastry flour
¼ cup carob powder
¾ cup chopped roasted peanuts
½ cup carob chips

Preheat oven to 350°. Lightly butter an 8" square pan.

In a small saucepan, over low heat, melt together peanut butter and butter until smooth and well blended. Remove from heat and cool. In a medium~sized bowl, beat eggs until light. Beat in honey, vanilla and salt. Blend in cooled peanut butter mixture. Stir in flour and carob powder; mix well. Fold in ½ cup of the chopped peanuts and carob chips. Pour batter into pan. Sprinkle top with remaining ¼ cup of peanuts.

Bake about 20 minutes, or until toothpick inserted in center comes out clean.

Cool before cutting.

Makes 16 brownies.

Wheat Germ Nugget Brownies

Lots of wholesome goodies packed into these nutritious bars.

1 cup honey
½ cup butter, softened
1 egg
1 teaspoon vanilla
1⅓ cups whole wheat pastry flour
½ teaspoon each salt and baking
   soda

½ teaspoon mace or nutmeg
   (choose your favorite)
1⅔ cups lightly toasted wheat germ
1 cup finely snipped dates
1 cup diced almonds
1 cup carob chips

Preheat oven to 350°. Butter a 13 x 9 x 2" pan.

In a large bowl, cream together honey, butter, egg and vanilla. In a small bowl, stir together flour, salt, baking soda and preferred spice. Gradually blend dry ingredients into creamed mixture. Stir in wheat germ, dates, almonds and carob chips; mix well. Spread batter evenly in pan.

Bake about 35 minutes, or until toothpick inserted in center comes out clean.

Cool completely. Cut carefully into bars with a sharp, serrated knife.
Makes 32 brownies.

Honey and Granola Brownies

Fabulous whole wheat and honey goodness. Top it off with a dusting of Powdered Coconut Sugar.

½ cup butter, softened
1 cup honey
1 egg
1 teaspoon vanilla
1 teaspoon grated fresh orange rind, packed (optional)
1⅓ cups whole wheat pastry flour
½ teaspoon each baking soda and salt
1 teaspoon cinnamon
1¾ cups granola
1 cup coconut
1 cup carob chips
Powdered Coconut Sugar (recipe follows)

Preheat oven to 350°. Butter a 13 x 9 x 2" pan.

In a large bowl, beat together butter, honey, egg and vanilla until smooth and creamy. Add optional orange rind. In a small bowl, combine flour, baking soda, salt and cinnamon. Gradually blend into creamed mixture; mix well. Stir in granola, coconut and carob chips.

Spread batter evenly in pan.

Bake 25 ~ 30 minutes, or until toothpick inserted in center comes out clean. Cool completely in pan.

Sprinkle top of brownies with Powdered Coconut Sugar, and cut into bars with a sharp knife.

Makes 32 brownies.

Powdered Coconut Sugar

Here lies a healthy alternative to powdered sugar. Just place desired amount of dried unsweetened coconut in a blender and process until finely ground. That's all! About ½ cup will yield enough to garnish a large pan of brownies. Store in a tightly covered container.

Blueberry Bran Brownies

Surprise! Blueberries for breakfast . . . and why not?

¼ cup butter
1 cup brown sugar, packed
1 egg
½ teaspoon vanilla
2 tablespoons dark molasses
1 cup whole wheat pastry flour
1 teaspoon baking powder
½ teaspoon nutmeg or cinnamon
   (whichever you are most fond of.)

⅛ teaspoon salt
¼ cup unprocessed bran
¾ cup fresh blueberries (or frozen,
   thawed and well drained)
¾ cup diced walnuts
½ cup dark or golden raisins

extra diced walnuts

- Preheat oven to 350.° Butter a 9" square pan.

- In a medium~sized saucepan, melt butter. Remove from heat and whisk in brown sugar. Beat in egg, then vanilla and molasses. Blend in flour, baking powder, spice, salt and bran until thoroughly moistened. Carefully fold in blueberries, walnuts and raisins. Pour into pan. Sprinkle top with extra diced walnuts, pressing down lightly.

- Bake 30~35 minutes, or until toothpick inserted in center comes out clean. Cut into bars while warm.

- Cool completely before removing from pan. Extra chewy and moist if re~frigerated.

Makes 20 brownies.

Carob Trail Mix Brownies

Moist with honey, crunchy with nuts, chewy with fruit.
For carob lovers.

½ cup butter, softened
⅔ cup honey
2 eggs
1 teaspoon vanilla
½ teaspoon salt
½ cup carob powder
⅔ cup whole wheat pastry flour, or unbleached white flour
1 teaspoon baking powder
¾ cup trail mix (carob chips, raisins, chopped dates, nuts, coconut, sunflower seeds, banana chips, etc.)

Preheat oven to 350°. Butter a 9" square pan.

With a wire whisk, cream together butter and honey. Beat in eggs, one at a time. Blend in vanilla and salt. In a separate bowl, stir together carob powder, flour and baking powder. Gradually stir dry ingredients into creamed mixture, blending well. Fold in trail mix. Spread evenly in pan.

Bake about 30 minutes, or until toothpick inserted in center comes out clean.

Cool completely in pan. Cut into bars. Extra delicious cold!
Makes 20 brownies.

～ Crunchy Breakfast Brownies ～

All we're missing here is the bacon!

1 cup brown sugar, packed
¼ cup honey
¼ cup peanut butter
¼ cup butter, softened
1 egg
1 teaspoon vanilla
1 cup flour (unbleached white or whole wheat pastry)
¼ cup unsweetened cocoa
¼ cup nonfat dry milk powder
½ teaspoon each baking soda and salt
1 cup granola
½ cup coconut
½ cup raisins
½ cup chocolate chips, carob chips or peanut butter chips
¼ cup wheat germ

～ extra granola ～

Preheat oven to 350.° Butter a 13 x 9 x 2" pan.

In a large bowl using an electric mixer, beat together brown sugar, honey, peanut butter, butter, egg and vanilla until smooth and creamy. In a small bowl, stir together flour, cocoa, dry milk powder, baking soda and salt. Gradually blend dry ingredients into creamed mixture. Thoroughly stir in 1 cup granola, coconut, raisins, chips and wheat germ. Mixture will be very stiff. Spread batter evenly in pan, using hands if necessary. Generously sprinkle top with extra granola, pressing down lightly.

Bake about 25 minutes, or until toothpick inserted in center comes out clean.

Cool in pan before cutting into bars.

Makes 32 brownies.

Granola Crunch Brownies

Chewy bars perfect for breakfast or a sturdy lunch box treat.

¼ cup butter, softened
¼ cup peanut butter
1 cup brown sugar, lightly packed
1 egg
1 teaspoon vanilla
1 ⅓ cups flour (whole wheat, white, or a combination)

½ teaspoon baking soda
½ teaspoon salt
¼ cup milk
1 ⅔ cups granola
⅔ cup each : chopped <u>dried fruit</u> (figs, dates, apricots, raisins), chopped toasted <u>peanuts</u> or <u>cashews</u>, <u>coconut</u>, and <u>peanut butter chips</u>

Preheat oven to 350° Butter a 13 x 9 x 2" pan.

Cream together butter, peanut butter, sugar, egg and vanilla. In a small bowl, stir together flour, baking soda and salt. Add dry ingredients to creamed mixture alternately with milk. Stir in granola, dried fruit, nuts, coconut and peanut butter chips; mix well. Spread batter evenly in pan.

Bake 25 ~ 30 minutes, or until toothpick inserted in center comes out clean.

Cool and cut.

Makes 32 brownies.

Carob Almond Chip Brownies

Surprisingly satisfying, and good for you, too!

4 eggs
2/3 cup safflower oil
½ cup honey
1 teaspoon vanilla
1 cup carob powder
½ cup whole wheat pastry flour, or unbleached white flour
1 teaspoon baking powder
½ teaspoon salt
¾ cup ground raw almonds
½ cup chopped almonds
½ cup carob chips

ground almonds for garnish

 Preheat oven to 325°. Butter a 9" square pan.

With a wire whisk, beat eggs until thick. Add oil, honey and vanilla; beat well. In a small bowl, stir together carob powder, flour, baking powder and salt. Blend into creamed mixture. Stir in ground almonds, chopped almonds and carob chips; mix well. Pour into pan.

Bake about 30 minutes, or until toothpick inserted in center comes out clean. Sprinkle hot brownie with more ground almonds. Cool completely.

Makes 20 brownies

Chocolatey Raisin Bran Brownies

For those of you who prefer dessert for breakfast. Or is it breakfast for dessert?

4 oz. unsweetened chocolate
½ cup butter
4 eggs
1½ cups honey
¼ cup frozen orange juice
    concentrate, thawed
1 teaspoon vanilla
½ teaspoon salt

1 cup flour (whole wheat pastry or
    unbleached white)
1⅓ cups raisin bran cereal, lightly
    crushed
½ cup each chocolate chips and
    wheat germ
1 cup raisins

~ extra crushed raisin bran cereal ~

- Preheat oven to 350°. Lightly butter a 13 x 9 x 2" pan.

- In a small saucepan, melt unsweetened chocolate and butter together over low heat; cool. In a large bowl, beat eggs well. Beat in honey until mixture is thick and smooth. Thoroughly stir in orange juice concentrate, vanilla and salt. Blend in melted chocolate mixture. Stir in flour, 1⅓ cups raisin bran, chocolate chips, wheat germ and raisins. Mix well. Pour batter into pan. Sprinkle top with extra lightly crushed cereal, pressing down lightly.

- Bake about 20 minutes, or until toothpick comes out clean.

- Cool before cutting. Makes 32 brownies.

118

Papaya Paradise Brownies

Macaroon-style bars, sweetened with honey, and over-flowing with coconut, dried papaya and cashews. Aloha!

2 cups raw oats
1 cup honey
½ cup butter, melted
1 egg
1 teaspoon vanilla

¾ teaspoon salt
2 cups grated coconut (use blender)
1 cup diced dried papaya
¾ cup finely chopped lightly
    toasted cashews

Preheat oven to 350°. Butter a 13 x 9 x 2" pan.

In a blender, process oats 1 cup at a time until powdery; set aside. In a large bowl, using a wire whisk, beat together honey, butter, egg, vanilla and salt until creamy. Add ground oats and beat well. Stir in coconut, papaya and cashews. Combine thoroughly. Spread batter evenly in pan.

Bake about 20 minutes, or until lightly golden and firm to the touch. Do not overbake.

Cool completely in pan. Chill thoroughly before cutting into bars.
Makes 32 brownies.

Frosted Peanut Butter and Carob Chip Brownies

Hearty, wholesome brownie fare. Makes an extra healthy snack paired up with a cold glass of milk.

½ cup butter, softened
½ cup honey
6 tablespoons peanut butter
1 egg
½ teaspoon vanilla
½ teaspoon baking soda
¼ teaspoon salt
1 cup whole wheat pastry flour
1 cup plain granola
1 cup carob chips

3 tablespoons carob powder
3 tablespoons honey
½ cup peanut butter
⅓ cup finely chopped roasted peanuts

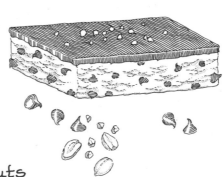

■ Preheat oven to 350°. Butter a 13 x 9 x 2" pan.

■ In a large bowl, using a wire whisk, beat together butter, ½ cup honey, 6 tablespoons peanut butter, egg and vanilla. Blend in baking soda, salt and flour; mix well. Stir in granola and carob chips. Spread batter evenly in pan.

 Bake about 20 minutes, or until golden and toothpick inserted in center comes out clean.

While brownies bake, combine carob powder and 3 tablespoons water in a small saucepan. Stir over low heat about 5 minutes, or until carob dissolves and mixture is smooth and slightly thickened. Remove from heat and blend in 3 tablespoons honey. Add ½ cup peanut butter; beat well. Carefully spread mixture over warm brownies, making an even layer. Sprinkle top with chopped peanuts, pressing down lightly.

 Cool in pan completely before cutting. Chill, or serve at room temperature.

Makes 32 brownies.

ELEGANT AND EXOTIC BROWNIES

Are you the adventurous type? Do you seek out unique and unusual experiences in life? Will you try anything once? Then this chapter was created just for you. Inside you will discover brownies beyond your wildest dreams. Ones baked with cheeses, creamy avocados, exotic liqueurs, and a host of other unexpected delicacies. Believe me, you won't be disappointed — just delighted.

Piña Colada Brownies

Now you can nibble on a favorite drink.

2 cups vanilla wafer crumbs, lightly packed
1 14~oz. can sweetened condensed milk
1 teaspoon rum extract
1 cup shredded coconut
1 cup chopped dried pineapple
½ cup slivered blanched almonds

∽extra shredded coconut ∾

Preheat oven to 350.° Butter a 9" square pan.

In a medium~sized bowl, stir together sweetened condensed milk and vanilla wafer crumbs; mix well. Blend in rum extract. Stir in 1 cup coconut, dried pineapple and almonds. Turn batter into pan. Lightly press extra coconut on top.

Bake about 25 minutes, or until done.

Cool completely. Cut into bars.

Makes 20 brownies.

～ Grasshopper Crème Brownies ～

An elegant sweet finish.

¼ cup butter
2 oz. unsweetened chocolate

2 tablespoons butter, softened
1 3-oz. package cream cheese, softened
¼ cup sugar
1 egg
1 tablespoon flour
1 teaspoon vanilla
green food coloring
½ cup chopped chocolate chips

2 eggs
1 cup sugar
¼ teaspoon salt
½ teaspoon vanilla
¼ cup crème de menthe
¾ cup flour

Preheat oven to 350°. Butter a 9" square pan.

In a small saucepan, melt together ¼ cup butter and unsweetened chocolate over low heat; set aside.

In a small bowl, beat together 2 tablespoons softened butter and cream cheese. Add ¼ cup sugar, 1 egg, 1 tablespoon flour and 1 teaspoon vanilla; beat until smooth and creamy. With food color, tint mixture a pale mint green, adding one drop at a time. Stir in chocolate chips.

In another bowl, using a wire whisk, beat 2 eggs until foamy. Beat in 1 cup sugar, salt and ½ teaspoon vanilla. Blend in crème de menthe, then melted chocolate mixture and ¾ cup flour. Combine thoroughly.

Pour ½ chocolate mint batter into pan, spreading evenly. Top with cream cheese mixture, making an even layer. Pour remaining choc~ olate mint batter over top. Very lightly swirl batters together with a knife.

Bake 35~40 minutes, or until done. Cool completely before cutting into bars.

Makes 20 brownies.

Deep Dark Espresso Brownies

Care for some dessert coffee?

¾ butter, melted
1 cup brown sugar, lightly packed
½ cup granulated sugar
1 teaspoon vanilla
¼ teaspoon salt
3 eggs

½ cup instant espresso coffee powder
  (not dissolved)
1 cup flour
¾ teaspoon baking powder
¾ cup chocolate chips

powdered sugar

 Preheat oven to 350°. Butter a 9" square pan.

In a large bowl, beat together melted butter and sugars. Add vanilla, salt and eggs. Beat until well blended. Stir in espresso powder, flour and baking powder, mixing until smooth. Fold in chocolate chips. Pour batter into pan.

Bake about 30 minutes, or until toothpick inserted in center comes out clean. Cool completely in pan.

Lightly dust top with powdered sugar, and cut into bars.
        Makes 20 brownies.

IMPORTED Espresso POWDER

Note: If the amount of coffee in this recipe overwhelms you, you can cut back by 2 or even 4 tablespoons of espresso powder. The brownies will still taste terrific!

Spiced Cranberry Walnut Brownies

Perfect on a cold December evening with a steamy mug of apple cider.

2 ½ cups graham cracker crumbs, lightly packed
1 teaspoon cinnamon
½ teaspoon nutmeg
¼ teaspoon allspice
1 14~oz. can sweetened condensed milk
¼ cup cranberry liqueur
1 cup chopped fresh cranberries
¾ cup diced walnuts
½ cup cut up golden raisins

~ powdered sugar ~

🍒 Preheat oven to 350°. Butter a 9" square pan.

🍒 In a large bowl, stir together graham cracker crumbs, cinnamon, nutmeg, and allspice. Thoroughly work in sweetened condensed milk. Batter will be very stiff. Blend in liqueur. Mix in cranberries, walnuts and raisins; combine well. Turn batter into pan, smoothing top to make even.

🍒 Bake about 25 minutes, or until toothpick inserted in center comes out clean. Cool completely.

🍒 Dust top generously with powdered sugar and cut into bars.

Makes 20 brownies.

French Buttercream Brownies

Smooth and velvety, with a captivating chocolate taste. Best aged a few hours before indulging (if you can handle temptation).

5 oz. unsweetened chocolate
1 cup butter, softened
1 ¾ cups brown sugar, packed
5 eggs
1½ teaspoons vanilla
½ cup Crème de Cacao
1¼ cups flour

Preheat oven to 350.° Butter a 13x9x2" pan.

In a small saucepan, melt chocolate over low heat. Set aside to cool. In a large bowl, cream together butter and sugar, using a wire whisk. Beat in eggs, one by one. Thoroughly blend in melted chocolate, then vanilla and Crème de Cacao. Stir in flour; mix well. Pour batter into pan.

Bake 20~25 minutes, or until toothpick inserted in center comes out clean.

Cool completely in pan. If possible, let brownies mellow overnight before cutting.

Makes 32 brownies.

Various Ways to Garnish and Enjoy:

- a light dusting of powdered sugar.
- 1 cup sliced, blanched almonds sprinkled on top just prior to baking.
- topped off with a scoop of French vanilla ice cream and crushed pecans (see "Sundaes").
- dollops of sweet whipped cream and chocolate curls applied just before serving.
- simply by themselves... they're absolute bliss!

Pralines 'n Cream Cheese Brownies

Brown sugar pralines can be found in specialty candy shops. A favorite southern sweet!

2 tablespoons butter, softened
1 3-oz. package cream cheese, softened
¼ cup sugar
1 egg
1 tablespoon flour
1 teaspoon vanilla
⅔ cup crushed praline candy

⅓ cup butter
1 cup brown sugar, packed
1 egg
1 teaspoon vanilla
1 cup flour
½ teaspoon each baking powder and salt
⅛ teaspoon baking soda

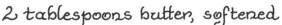

🥜 **P**reheat oven to 350°. Lightly butter a 9" square pan.

🥜 **I**n a small bowl, beat 2 tablespoons soft butter with cream cheese until fluffy. Beat in ¼ cup sugar, 1 egg, 1 tablespoon flour and 1 teaspoon vanilla. Stir in candy; set aside.

🍪 **I**n a small saucepan, melt ⅓ cup butter; remove from heat. Stir in brown sugar. Beat in egg and 1 teaspoon vanilla. Blend in flour, baking powder, salt and baking soda; mix well.

🍪 **S**pread half of brown sugar batter evenly in pan. Spread cream cheese mixture over top. Drop spoonfuls of remaining brown sugar batter on top of cream cheese layer. Swirl top of batter lightly with a knife to marbleize.

🍪 **B**ake 40~45 minutes, or until toothpick inserted in center comes out clean. Cool completely before cutting into bars.

Makes 20 brownies.

Chocolate Kahlúa Mousse Brownies

Only one word to describe these . . . sinful.

10 oz. semisweet chocolate
6 eggs, separated and at room temperature
½ teaspoon vanilla
¼ cup sugar
2 tablespoons flour
¼ teaspoon salt
½ cup butter, softened
2 tablespoons Kahlúa (coffee liqueur)

~ sweetened whipped cream and shaved chocolate for garnish ~

Preheat oven to 375.° Butter a 13 x 9 x 2" pan.

Melt chocolate over very low heat; set aside to cool. In a large bowl with electric mixer, beat egg yolks until light and lemon yellow. Beat in vanilla, 1 tablespoon of the sugar, flour, salt and butter until very creamy. Thoroughly blend in melted chocolate and Kahlúa. In a separate bowl, beat egg whites until soft peaks form. Continue beating, adding remaining sugar, until stiff. Fold into chocolate mixture. Turn batter into prepared pan. Bake about 20 minutes, or until center is just set.

Cool completely, then chill. Cut into bars.

Decorate with whipped cream and shaved chocolate; serve on dessert plates.

Makes 24 brownies.

～ Luscious Avocado Nut Brownies ～

Marvel your guests with these chewy, chunky, pale green bars of paradise.

¾ cup butter, melted
1 ½ cups sugar
2 eggs
½ cup mashed ripe avocado
1 teaspoon vanilla
¼ teaspoon salt

¾ teaspoon baking powder
1 cup flour
½ cup lightly toasted coconut
½ cup finely snipped dates
½ cup chopped macadamia nuts

～ powdered sugar ～

- Preheat oven to 350°. Butter a 9" square pan.

- In a large bowl, beat together melted butter and sugar. Beat in eggs, one by one. Blend in avocado, vanilla and salt. Thoroughly stir in baking powder and flour. Fold in coconut, dates and macadamia nuts; mix well. Spread batter evenly in pan.

- Bake 25~30 minutes, or until toothpick inserted in center comes out clean. Cool in pan.

- Dust top with powdered sugar and cut into bars.

Makes 20 brownies.

～ Italian Ricotta Brownies ～

All those Italian favorites in a melt~in~your~
mouth chocolate brownie...fantastico!

½ cup butter, softened
1 cup sugar
1 egg
1 cup ricotta cheese
1 teaspoon vanilla
¼ cup Amaretto Liqueur
2 cups flour
½ cup unsweetened cocoa
½ teaspoon _each_ baking soda and salt
¾ cup chopped chocolate chips
½ cup diced mixed candied fruits
½ cup sliced blanched almonds
Amaretto Fudge Frosting (recipe follows)
～ extra sliced almonds ～

Amaretto Fudge Frosting

sliced almonds

candied fruit

chocolate chips

🍫 Preheat oven to 375°. Butter a 13 x 9 x 2" pan.

🍫 In a large bowl, cream butter and sugar until light and fluffy.
Beat in egg, then ricotta and vanilla. Blend in Amaretto. In a
small bowl, stir together flour, cocoa, baking soda and salt.

Gradually beat dry ingredients into creamed mixture. Stir in chocolate chips, candied fruit and ½ cup almonds. Spread batter evenly in pan.

Bake about 20 minutes, or until toothpick inserted in center comes out clean. Cool completely in pan on wire rack.

Frost top of brownies with Amaretto Fudge Frosting, and sprinkle with extra sliced almonds. Let frosting set before cutting into bars.

Makes 32 brownies.

Amaretto Fudge Frosting

¼ cup butter	¼ teaspoon salt
1 cup granulated sugar	2 cups powdered sugar
1 cup chocolate chips	1 teaspoon vanilla
½ cup milk	Amaretto liqueur

In a medium-sized saucepan, combine butter, granulated sugar, chocolate chips, milk and salt. Bring to a boil, stirring constantly. Simmer 3 minutes and remove from heat. Blend in powdered sugar and vanilla. Beat until creamy. Add a small amount of Amaretto (1~2 tablespoons) to achieve a good consistency for spreading. Frost.

Brandied Peaches and Cream Brownies

A creamy peach ribbon surrounded by chewy golden batter.

2 tablespoons butter, softened
1 3-oz. package cream cheese, softened
¼ cup sugar
1 egg
1 ½ tablespoons flour
½ teaspoon vanilla
1 tablespoon peach brandy
1 cup finely chopped dried peaches

⅓ cup butter
1 cup brown sugar, packed
1 egg
½ teaspoon vanilla
1 tablespoon peach brandy
1 cup flour
½ teaspoon each baking powder and salt
⅛ teaspoon baking soda
½ cup diced walnuts

Preheat oven to 350.° Butter a 9" square pan.

In a small bowl, beat together 2 tablespoons softened butter and cream cheese until fluffy. Beat in ¼ cup sugar, 1 egg and 1½ tablespoons flour. Thoroughly stir in ½ teaspoon vanilla, 1 tablespoon peach brandy and dried peaches; set aside.

In a small saucepan, melt ⅓ cup butter. Remove from heat and stir in 1 cup brown sugar. Beat in remaining egg, ½ teaspoon vanilla and 1 tablespoon peach brandy. Blend in 1 cup flour, baking powder, salt and baking soda; mix well. Fold in walnuts.

Spread ½ brown sugar batter evenly in pan. Spread cream cheese mixture over top, covering batter completely. Spoon dollops of remaining brown sugar batter over cream cheese layer in a scattered pattern. Lightly swirl top batters together with a knife.

Bake 40~45 minutes, or until toothpick inserted in center comes out clean.

Cool in pan. Chill for easier cutting.

Makes 20 brownies

BROWNIE CREATIONS and SPECIALTIES

...TO PLEASE EVERYONE

❧ Frozen ❧ BROWNIE~WICHES

Here's a treat no one can resist. It's a slab of your favorite ice cream sandwiched between two thin brownie bars, frozen and ready for the asking. The best part — it's so easy and so impressive. Children's birth~ day parties become extra special when each youngster is handed an in~ dividually wrapped treat that combines so many favorite flavors into one. With all the brownie recipes in this book, and all the ice cream flavors in the world to choose from, you can create quite a tempting variety of frozen sandwiches. Here are a few pointers to keep in mind, along with a basic brownie ice cream sandwich~making pro~ cedure.

1. Use a brownie recipe calling for an 8" or 9" pan only, but bake the brownies in a 15 ½ x 10 ½ x 1" jelly roll pan. These brownie bars need to be quite thin in order to freeze to the proper consistency.

2. To use a 13 x 9 x 2" recipe, cut the recipe in half and bake as directed in a jelly roll pan.

3. Cool baked brownies thoroughly before cutting into bars for sand~ wiches.

4. Buy your ice cream in ½~gallon brick form. It slices easily, and makes professional looking bars.

5. Work quickly. The ice cream melts fast, especially once it's cut. Have your brownie bars ready to go and freezer space already cleared.

6. First, place just made ice cream sandwiches in a single layer on a waxed paper~lined cookie sheet to firm up. After they are partially frozen, trim bars to make even, if necessary; dip in Crunchies, if desired (see #7); wrap in foil or plastic wrap and freeze until solid.

7. Feel free to dip partially frozen sandwiches in Crunchies (chocolate chips, nuts, granola, etc.). Dip sides of ice cream only and refreeze quickly.

8. Mix and match ice cream flavors and brownie recipes wisely. Don't go overboard. A simpler brownie with a fancy ice cream and vice versa.

9. Brownie bars are thin and delicate. Handle with care.

THE PROCEDURE

1 brownie recipe (use a recipe that calls for an 8" or 9" pan)

½ gallon brick ice cream (your favorite)

Crunchies, optional (details follow)

Preheat oven to 350.° Butter a 15½ x 10½ x 1" jelly roll pan. Prepare brownie batter as directed in recipe. Spread batter evenly in pan. Bake about 20 minutes, or until toothpick inserted in center comes out clean and brownie is semi~firm to the touch. Cool completely in pan on wire rack. With a sharp knife, cut brownie lengthwise into 3 equal pieces. Cut each piece crosswise into 10 bars. You will have 30 brownies of uniform size.

Remove ice cream from freezer, and discard carton. With a large, sharp knife, cut ice cream crosswise into 3 even pieces. Cut each piece into 5 (1") slices. Working quickly, place each ice cream slice between 2 brownie bars, with shiny brownie top exposed on each side. Immediately place bars on a waxed paper~lined cookie sheet and freeze until semi~ hard (about 1 hour). Remove bars one at a time, trim to make even, if necessary, and dip in Crunchies° (a purely optional addition). Wrap in~ dividually in plastic or foil, and freeze until solid ~2 hours or longer. To eat: just unwrap and enjoy! Makes 15 BROWNIE~WICHES.

° Crunchies:

~ toasted coconut
~ granola
~ chips! (chocolate, butterscotch, peanut butter or carob~whole or chopped)
~ trail mix
~ nonpareils
~ chocolate sprinkles
~ chopped nuts

<u>Two Notes</u>: 1. Do not use Chocolate Kahlua Mousse Brownies or any <u>unbaked</u> brownie in this recipe.

2. Omit frosting when making these dessert sandwiches.

Shapely Brownie Celebrations!

Everyone is familiar with a brownie bar or square, but how about brownie rounds, stars, or even Santas? Just turn your favorite cookie cutters loose on a large panful of brownies—it's that simple. These brownies make delicious holiday desserts or gifts, and are even better when frosted and decorated with nuts, raisins, or other crunchy morsels. You can use an ornamental frosting recipe piped through a pastry bag to outline each shape, too (very professional looking).

The brownies have to be thin—use an 8" or 9" recipe and bake in a 15½ x 10½ x 1" jelly roll pan. Let brownies cool completely in pan, then with a sharp cookie cutter, cut out each desired shape and remove carefully with a large spatula. Frost and decorate as desired. They can be successfully frozen for future desserts, too. For a more de-tailed baking procedure, see "Frozen Brownie-wiches".

Below, you will find some creative ideas for incorporating these shapes into your holiday celebrations. After all, what's a holiday without brownies?

1. Gingerbread Graham Cracker Brownies cut into gingerbread boys, outlined in ornamental frosting and decorated with raisins or currants (for children's Christmas parties).

2. Chocolate Mint Brownies cut into four-leaf clovers. Spread Peppermint Cream Frosting over tops and omit Sweet Chocolate Glaze (for St. Patrick's Day).

3. Pumpkin Praline Brownies cut into jack~o~lanterns. Frost with Creamy Cream Cheese Frosting (tinted orange) and make faces with nuts and raisins (for Halloween).

4. Chocolate Cherry Cordial Brownies cut into hearts, frosted in pink, and decorated with cherries for Valentine's Day.

5. Fudgy Fruitcake Brownies cut into Santas, trees, or reindeer, frosted in white buttercream, and decorated with candied cherries and nuts (for "the holidays").

6. Lemon Poppyseed Brownies cut into stars or flags, frosted in white and decorated with red and blue nonpareils (for July 4th).

Note: Chop nuts and other crunchy things rather finely before adding to the batter. The batter will spread thinly and evenly, thus avoiding unnecessary chunkiness.

LEFTOVER PIECES OF BROWNIE?

~ Cut into small pieces, fold into softened ice cream and refreeze.
~ Crumble and use as a dry sundae topping.
~ When cut into tiny squares, they are the perfect size for small children.
~ Dry briefly in oven, grind in blender, and use to make a crumb piecrust. (Will not work with unbaked, frosted, or Chocolate Kahlua Mousse Brownies.)
~ Layer into Parfait or Goblet sundaes.
~ Nibble while you decide what to do.

MORE BROWNIE SPECIALTIES

It seems as if most of the more exclusive restaurants and eateries have some sort of dessert based on a chocolate brownie. It may be topped with ice cream, hot fudge, whipped cream and cherries. It may be served hot like a pie, or with a thick layer of chocolate frosting. Creatively speak~ing, there are no limitations, as you will see. From outrageous sundaes, to pies, parfaits and even orgies (yes, orgies!), there's a brownie original for everyone.

The brownie specialties that follow are guaranteed to rival those of any fancy restaurant, not to mention bringing <u>oohs</u> and <u>ahhs</u> from those who indulge in them.

∽ The Brownie Sundae ∽

Any brownie can be made into a beautiful sundae, with the help of your favorite ice cream, sauces and toppings. Start with a large brown~ie square, top with a generous scoop or slab of ice cream (1 pint for every 3~4 sundaes), spoon on your favorite sauce (¼ cup per person), add some real whipped cream, an ample sprinkling of nuts and a large stemmed cherry. There you have the basic recipe. For a long list of mind~boggling sundae creations, see pages 146~147.

The Brownie Banana Split

Here's a delicious variation of a most popular American tradition. For each serving, place 2 brownie squares in the bottom of a large banana split boat. Slice a medium-sized ripe banana lengthwise and place on opposite sides of dish. Top brownies with 2 or 3 scoops of your favorite ice cream, some sliced fresh strawberries, marshmallow sauce and chocolate or hot fudge sauce. Spoon or pipe whipped cream generously over top, and sprinkle with nuts, coconut, granola, or other crunchy delights. Lastly, place a sweet stemmed maraschino cherry on top of each ice cream scoop. Now, eat very quickly, before it all melts!!

Brownie	Ice Cream
Sour Cream Chocolate Chip	Mint Chip
S'More	Chocolate Chip
Mocha Almond Fudge	Coffee
Mandarin Chocolate Chip	Orange Sherbet
Banana Chocolate Chip	Strawberry
Chocolate Pudding	Chocolate Chip
Chewy Butterscotch	Vanilla
Peanut Butter and Banana	French Vanilla
Carob Trail Mix	Honey Vanilla
Chocolate Amaretto Crunch	French Vanilla
Chocolate Peanut Butter Chip	Chocolate Chip
Pralines 'n Cream Cheese	Vanilla
Fudgy Macadamia Nut	French Vanilla
Oatmeal Date Nut	Chocolate
Spiced Apple	French Vanilla
Grasshopper Creme	Vanilla
Fudgy Fruitcake	Spumoni
Wheat Germ Nugget	Frozen Yogurt

Sauce	Whipped Cream	Nuts/Crunchies	Garnish
Chocolate		Shaved Chocolate	Cherries
Marshmallow		Graham Cracker Crumbs	Cherries
Hot Fudge		Toasted Almonds	Cherries
Chocolate		Chocolate Sprinkles	Orange Segments
Chocolate		Chopped Walnuts	Sliced Bananas
Hot Fudge	Whipped Cream	Whole Pecans	Cherries
Butterscotch		Toasted Coconut	Pineapple Chunks
Chocolate		Chopped Peanuts	Sliced Bananas
Crushed Berries		Granola	Whole Pitted Dates
Almond Liqueur	Whipped Cream	Toasted Almonds	Cherries
Hot Fudge		Chopped Peanuts	Cherries
Caramel		Crushed Praline Candy	Cherries
Chocolate		Toasted Macadamia Nuts	Pineapple Chunks
Caramel		Chopped Walnuts	Sliced Dates
Butterscotch	Whipped Cream	Toasted Coconut	Cherries
Mint Liqueur		Chocolate Curls	Cherries
Favorite Liqueur		Walnut Halves	Candied Cherries
Crushed Berries	Whipped Cream	Carob Chips	Chopped Dates

147

⌒ Brownie Mud Pie ⌒

Bake a batch of brownies~but in a pie pan. Fill it with creamy ice cream, top it with a layer of thick fudge sauce (or any sauce for that matter), pile on some real whipped cream, and sprinkle with your favorite crunchy toppings. Cut into wedges and serve on a chilled plate with a chilled fork. Another dessert accomplishment! So many mouthwatering flavors and textures rolled into one...chewy, creamy, nutty, crunchy!

YOU WILL NEED:

1 brownie recipe that calls for an 8" or 9" pan~ or cut a 13 x 9 x 2" recipe in half. Bake the brownies in a 9"or 10" pyrex pie plate (lower oven temperature by 25°).

1 quart slightly softened ice cream~flavor ideas follow

1½ cups fudge sauce ~ cold or room temperature (or another sauce of your choice)

2 cups sweetened whipped cream

Garnishes ~ toasted coconut, chocolate curls, nut halves, cherries, etc.

Cool brownie completely in pie plate on wire rack. Fill with softened ice cream, slightly building up center. Freeze until firm, about 1½ hours. Spread fudge sauce carefully over top, sealing in ice cream and making layer as even and smooth as possible. Freeze again. To serve: pipe or spoon whipped cream generously in a circle where ice cream and brownie meet. Pile more whipped cream into center of pie. Dec~ orate whipped cream with crunchy garnishes and slice into 6 to 8 portions with a sharp serving knife. Serves 6~8.

Three IMPORTANT Notes:

1. If brownie base is too hard to cut through, let pie soften at room temperature 10 min~ utes or longer.

2. When spreading batter in pan, build up sides to form a nice crust (providing batter is not too thin) to help accommodate the ice cream. Bake.

3. You can use an unbaked brownie recipe, too. Just press batter in pie plate, form~ ing a shell as you go. Chill brownie crust until firm, as original recipe directs.

real whipped cream

maraschino cherry

sliced toasted almonds

fudge sauce

brownie crust

chocolate ripple ice cream

MUD PIE COMBINATIONS:

~ Mocha Almond Fudge Brownies (half a recipe), coffee ice cream, fudge sauce, toasted almonds.

~ Chocolate Peanut Chip Brownies, chocolate chip ice cream, chocolate sauce, chopped toasted peanuts and chocolate sprinkles.

~ Chewy Coffee Chip Brownies, chocolate ice cream, caramel sauce, walnut halves.

~ Chocolate Cherry Cordial Brownies, French vanilla ice cream, fudge sauce, slivered almonds, maraschino cherries.

~ Chocolate Pudding Brownies, strawberry ice cream, chocolate sauce, chocolate or colored sprinkles.

~ Maple Walnut Brownies, chocolate chip ice cream, caramel sauce, toasted coconut, chopped walnuts.

~ Peanut Butter and Carob Fudge Brownies, honey vanilla ice cream, carob sauce, chopped toasted peanuts and carob chips.

~ Burnt Almond Chip Brownies, French vanilla ice cream, caramel sauce, chopped toasted almonds and chocolate chips.

~ Orange Almond Crunch Brownies, chocolate chip ice cream, chocolate or fudge sauce, sliced toasted almonds and candied orange peel.

~ Fudgy Macadamia Nut Brownies, mint chip ice cream, fudge sauce, toasted macadamia nuts, chocolate curls.

Parfaits and Goblets

Parfaits and goblets are layered sundaes, a little more elegant than ordinary sundaes, but just as easy to prepare. Parfait glasses are tall and thin, appealing to daintier eaters; goblets are heavier, hold more, and attract heartier appetites.

The ingredients consist basically of layers of brownies, ice cream and sauce, with a topping of whipped cream, nuts and a cherry. But you can also use cookie crumbs, pudding, fruit, or even crunchies like nuts and coconut. For a long list of brownie~ice cream-sauce combinations, see the section on Brownie Sundaes. Following, are a few "Mouth~watering Suggestions" for these delicious layered desserts. It doesn't take much effort to impress a dinner guest...just offer 'em one of these!

FOR PARFAITS (per serving)

- ~ 1 average brownie (halved and layered)
- ~ ½ cup (about) ice cream or pudding
- ~ 2 tablespoons sauce
- ~ sweetened whipped cream, nuts, cherry for garnish

FOR GOBLETS (per serving)

~ 2 brownies (each cut in half and placed around sides of goblet or layered with other ingredients)

~ 1 ~1½ cups ice cream or pudding

~ ¼ cup sauce

~ sweetened whipped cream, nuts (or other crunchies), cherry

Note: Glass sizes vary, thus all measurements are approximate.

MOUTH~WATERING SUGGESTIONS

1. Chocolate Mint Brownie(s) layered with mint chip ice cream and chocolate sauce, topped with whipped cream, chocolate sprinkles and a cherry.

2. Peanut Butter and Banana Brownie(s) layered with chocolate pudding, whipped cream, toasted peanuts and banana slices.

3. Double Rocky Road Brownie(s) layered with chocolate chip ice cream and marshmallow sauce, topped with whipped cream, crushed walnuts and a cherry.

4. German Chocolate Brownie(s) layered with French vanilla ice cream and hot fudge, topped off with whipped cream, toasted coconut and a stemmed maraschino.

5. Sour Cream Chocolate Chip Brownie(s) layered with creamy vanilla pudding and chocolate sauce, topped with whipped cream, chocolate curls and a cherry.

6. Carrot Coconut Brownie(s) layered with vanilla ice cream and butterscotch sauce, topped with whipped cream, toasted coconut and fresh pineapple chunks. Fantastic!

7. Deep Dark Espresso Brownie(s) layered with coffee ice cream and hot fudge, topped off with whipped cream, shaved chocolate and a cherry.

8. Carob Almond Chip Brownie(s) layered with honey vanilla ice cream or frozen yogurt and crushed fresh berries, topped with whipped cream, carob chips and a fresh cherry. Mmm!

9. English Toffee Brownie(s) layered with chocolate ice cream and caramel sauce, topped with whipped cream, chopped walnuts and a cherry.

10. Orange Almond Crunch Brownie(s) layered with vanilla ice cream and chocolate sauce, topped off with whipped cream, toasted almonds and fresh orange segments. Wow!

Do-It-Yourself
⌁ Brownie Sundae Buffet ⌁

Want a guarantee that the next party you give will be one long remembered by everyone? Then by all means, include a Do-It-Yourself Brownie Sundae Buffet. There's nothing quite like it. Each guest concocts a personalized sundae from a scrumptious array of homemade brownies, sauces, fruits and toppings you provide. And it's embarrassingly easy: just set everything out on your buffet table and let 'em dig in. People of all ages (from small children to grandparents) enjoy creating their own spectacular desserts. You can even build an entire party around this one idea. Following, are some helpful guidelines to keep in mind, along with some fabulous menu suggestions. So let yourself go, and have some fun!

* Allow about 2 brownies for every adult participant.

* Cut brownies into large bars, suitable for a large scoop or slab of ice cream and some toppings.

* You may serve only 6 guests from an 8" pan of brownies. Better bake a little extra, just in case.

* For children's parties, cut brownies into smaller portions and

use a small ice cream scoop when serving. Offer both large and small brownie squares when there are children and adults at the same party.

* Cut brownies into different and exciting shapes with a sharp cookie cutter. (See the section "Shapely Brownie Celebrations!")

* Offer your guests more than one type of brownie, especially for a large gathering; some caky, some fudgy.

* Hot fudge is the preferred topping, but don't hesitate to exper~iment with others. Offer 2 or 3 sauces.

* Whipped cream can be made ahead of time, piped or spooned into a serving bowl, and chilled until dessert time.

* Put gooey sauces and toppings in small pitchers. You can label them "chocolate," "hot caramel," etc.

* Dry toppings like nuts and granola can be placed in indi~vidual serving bowls or a divided dish, with a teaspoon for each.

* Leave the stems on cherries. They look nicer that way.

* Scoop out ice cream ahead of time if you wish. Lay ice cream balls on a tray in your freezer for a brief period to harden, pile into a large bowl, cover, and replace in the freezer until serving time. Try using 2 or more flavors, and serve with large spoons or pretty salad tongs.

* Piping hot coffee and glasses of icy cold milk make great go~withs.

BROWNIE BUFFET #1

Banana Chocolate Chip and Chocolate Butterscotch Swirl Brownies

chocolate chip and French vanilla ice creams

chocolate and hot butterscotch sauces

whipped cream

cherries, chocolate sprinkles, sliced bananas (dipped in lemon juice) and chopped walnuts

BROWNIE BUFFET #2

Peanut Brittle Cream and Mocha Almond Fudge Brownies

vanilla and chocolate ice creams

hot fudge and caramel sauces

whipped cream

chopped toasted peanuts, chocolate chips and cherries

BROWNIE BUFFET #3

Chocolate Marshmallow Creme and Chewy Coffee Chip Brownies
chocolate ripple and French vanilla ice creams
marshmallow and hot fudge sauces
whipped cream
toasted coconut, milk chocolate chips and cherries

BROWNIE BUFFET #4

Carrot Coconut and Fudgy Macadamia Nut Brownies
chocolate chip and French vanilla ice creams
caramel and chocolate sauces
whipped cream
fresh pineapple chunks, coconut chips, toasted macadamias
and chocolate covered raisins

BROWNIE BUFFET #5

Honey and Granola and Peanut Butter and Carob Fudge Brownies
frozen yogurt and honey vanilla ice cream
carob sauce and crushed strawberries
whipped cream
carob chips, granola and chopped peanuts

The Brownie Orgy Experience

...for very special company

Here's an alternative to the Do-It-Yourself Brownie Sundae Buffet. How about just 1 brownie sundae, so big and luscious it will serve 10, 20, or even 50 delighted guests? It's a masterpiece you create in your own kitchen with a variety of goodies to please everyone. You literally build a dessert mountain~with brownies, ice cream, and all sorts of delectable toppings. Here you will find sample orgies and a detailed procedure for creating one of your own. As usual, there are no limitations (only your imagination!). But work quickly and artfully, because as you already know, ice cream melts fast!

PROCEDURE:

Use a large, pretty serving platter for this dessert. You will need a few large utensils so several guests can serve themselves at the same time. Have forks, spoons and extra napkins ready for your participants. Per person, plan on 2 small brownies or 1 large one, 2 moderate scoops of ice cream and about 1/4 cup sauce. These amounts vary, of course, according to what extravagant fruits and toppings you ladle on. After building the basic brownie~ice cream~sauce sundae, you are then ready to decorate with whipped cream, fruit chunks, chopped nuts and an assortment of other crunchy, high calorie good~

ies. Here goes . . .

Around the edge of your platter, lay a ring of brownies, sides touch~ing. Scoop a circle of ice cream just inside the brownies, and slightly overlapping them. Now stand some brownies, side by side, just inside your ice cream ring and fill in with more scoops. Pile extra ice cream in the center to build up your mountain, alternating flavors of both ice cream and brownies (reserve a few brownies for deco~ration). At this point you may wish to temporarily place the platter in your freezer and collect all sauces and toppings for the finale.

When ready to serve, pour on the sauces (use warm, not hot sauces), then with a pastry bag, pipe whipped cream decoratively in wreaths around the scoops of ice cream. Scatter mouth~watering fruit chunks all over, tucking them neatly into the whipped cream. Generously sprinkle the entire mountain with all your dry toppings, and last but not least cut those reserved brownies into ½" sticks and place them ever~so~gently into the whipped cream. Now at last, you have created an original edible masterpiece (be sure a camera is ready). Have a trusted friend help you carry the platter to your famished guests. Any leftovers can be frozen and enjoyed throughout the week(s) to come.

Variation:

Instead of pouring on the sauces, serve them in large goblets so guests can pick and choose. Surround the goblets with ice cream, brownies and whipped cream for a nice effect.

∾ SAMPLE ORGY MENUS ∾

BROWNIES: Ultimate Fudge and Peanut Butter and Banana
ICE CREAMS: chocolate chip, coffee and rocky road
SAUCES: fudge and caramel
WHIPPED CREAM: lots!
FRUITS: banana spears, whole strawberries and orange segments.
DRY TOPPINGS: chocolate covered raisins, banana chips and
    chopped walnuts.

BROWNIES: Chocolate Marshmallow Cream, Pralines 'n Cream
    Cheese and Oatmeal Date Nut
ICE CREAMS: butter pecan, chocolate chip and strawberry
SAUCES: marshmallow, chocolate and butterscotch
WHIPPED CREAM: (same as above)
FRUITS: fresh berries, pineapple chunks and cherries
DRY TOPPINGS: toasted coconut, pecan halves, golden raisins
    and chocolate chips

BROWNIES: Fudgy Fruitcake, Divinity Fudge and Grasshopper
    Creme
ICE CREAMS: mint chip and French vanilla
SAUCES: chocolate and marshmallow
WHIPPED CREAM: of course
FRUITS: candied pineapple, cherries and fresh grapes
DRY TOPPINGS: white coconut, walnut halves and chocolate curls

<u>BROWNIES</u>: Papaya Paradise, Granola Crunch and Honey Fudge

<u>ICE CREAMS</u>: frozen yogurt and honey vanilla

<u>SAUCES</u>: carob and crushed fresh strawberries

<u>WHIPPED CREAM</u>: yes!

<u>FRUITS</u>: whole pitted dates, fresh pineapple chunks and fresh cherries

<u>DRY TOPPINGS</u>: carob covered raisins, toasted coconut and chopped cashews

THE BROWNIE ORGY EXPERIENCE

Some Suggested Fruits, Sauces and Toppings

∽ For All Sorts of Sundae Creations ∽

FRUITS:

~ Bananas (spears or chunks)
~ Peaches, plums, nectarines (fresh, ripe slices)
~ Grapes (seedless; red or green)
~ Kiwi (thinly sliced)
~ Blueberries, raspberries, boysenberries (for that elegant touch)
~ Pineapple (fresh or canned unsweetened)
~ Apricot (fresh halves)
~ Melons (honeydew or cantaloupe in balls or chunks)
~ Strawberries (whole with stems or sliced)
~ Cherries (with stems; fresh or maraschino)
~ Oranges (fresh or canned segments, or fresh sliced wheels)

SAUCES:

~ Chocolate
~ Butterscotch
~ Marshmallow
~ Caramel
~ Assorted liqueurs

~ Fudge (hot, warm or cold)
~ Carob
~ Pure maple syrup
~ Honey

DRY TOPPINGS:

~ Chips (chocolate, peanut butter, carob, butterscotch)
~ Coconut (white or lightly toasted; shredded, flaked or chips)
~ Sprinkles (chocolate or multicolored nonpareils)
~ Chocolate curls
~ Shaved chocolate
~ Dates (pitted; whole, sliced or chopped)
~ Chocolate or carob covered nuts and raisins
~ Nuts (whole or chopped, raw or toasted)
~ Granola
~ Banana chips
~ Dried currants or raisins
~ Dried apricot, papaya or pineapple pieces
~ Marshmallows (miniature)
~ Chocolate bar (broken into chunks)
~ Cookie crumbs or crumbled brownies
~ Trail mix
~ Seeds (pumpkin, poppy, sunflower)
~ Peppermints or buttermints (crushed or whole)
~ Jellybeans
~ Candied fruit peels (orange or lemon)
~ Coffee (ground, uncooked)

Index to Recipes

The Brownies

Banana Chocolate Chip, 41
Banana Oatmeal Chip, 107
Black Bottom, 61
Blueberry Bran, 112
Brandied Peaches and Cream, 136
Burnt Almond Chip, 74
Butter Rum Raisin, 57
Capuccino Chip, 54
Caramel Coconut Pecan, 98
Carob Almond Chip, 117
Carob Trail Mix, 113
Carrot Coconut, 80
Cherry Bonbon, 69
Chewy Butterscotch, 91
Chewy Coffee Chip, 71
Chinese Almond, 86
Chocolate Amaretto Crunch, 29
Chocolate Butterscotch Swirl, 44
Chocolate Caramel Turtle, 24
Chocolate Cherry Cordial, 49, 143
Chocolate Kahlua Mousse, 132
Chocolate Mint, 30–31

Chocolate Peanut Butter Chip, 40
Chocolate Pudding, 45
Chocolatey Raisin Bran, 118
Chunky Black Walnut, 103
Chunky Mincemeat, 88
Cinnamon Fudge, 53
Cinnamon Honey Graham Cracker, 76
Coconut Key Lime, 83
Coconut Macaroon Chip, 70
Coconut Marshmallow Creme, 38
Cream Cheese Swirl, 46
Crunchy Breakfast, 114
Crunchy Peanut Butter and Jelly, 90
Crunchy Vanilla Pecan, 66
Deep Dark Espresso, 126
Divinity Fudge, 58
Double Chocolate Malted, 59
Double Chocolate Peanut, 26
Double Rocky Road, 56
English Toffee, 67
French Buttercream, 128
Frosted Peanut Butter and Carob Chip,
    120
Fruity Spumoni, 73

Fudgy Fruitcake, 42
Fudgy Macadamia Nut, 36
Fudgy Raspberry, 33
Fudgy Strawberry, 33
German Chocolate, 50
Gingerbread Graham Cracker, 82
Golden Eggnog, 102
Granola Crunch, 116
Grasshopper Creme, 124
Heavenly Ambrosia, 60
Honey and Granola, 110
Honey Fudge, 106
Honeycomb Chip, 77
Irish Coffee, 99
Italian Ricotta, 134
Lemon Poppyseed, 95
Lemony Tutti-Frutti, 87
Luscious Avocado Nut, 133
Mandarin Chocolate Chip, 27
Maple Walnut, 72
Milk Chocolate, 48
Mocha Almond Fudge, 37
Oatmeal Date Nut, 68
Orange Almond Crunch, 65

165

Papaya Paradise, 119
Peanut Brittle Cream, 100
Peanut Butter and Banana, 79
Peanut Butter and Carob Fudge, 108
Peanut Butter Cup, 75
Piña Colada, 123
Pistachio Chocolate Swirl, 52
Pralines 'n Cream Cheese, 130
Pumpkin Praline, 84
Sesame Honey, 104
S'More, 63
Sour Cream Chocolate Chip, 23
Spiced Apple, 96
Spiced Cranberry Walnut, 127
Spicy Chocolate Chip, 34
Toasted Cashew, 94
Turkish Apricot Creme, 92
Ultimate Fudge, 35
Wheat Germ Nugget, 109
White Chocolate Almond, 62
White Chocolate Chip, 43
Yogurt Almond, 32
Zucchini Nut, 28

Frostings and Toppings

Amaretto Fudge Frosting, 135
Brandy Butter Icing, 89
Caramel Syrup, 25
Chocolate Cream Frosting, 39
Coconut Pecan Topping, 51
Creamy Cream Cheese Frosting, 85
Orange Cream Cheese Frosting, 81
Peppermint Cream Frosting, 31
Powdered Coconut Sugar, 111
Sweet Chocolate Glaze, 31
Vanilla Cream Icing, 97

Brownie-Based Treats

cookies, 142–143
ice cream sandwiches, 17, 139–141
parfaits, 17, 151–153
pies/piecrust, 143, 148–150
sundaes, 144–147, 154–157, 158–163

Index to Special Brownie Ingredients and Flavorings

almonds/almond extract/Amaretto, 27, 29, 30, 32, 33, 37, 46, 49, 52, 60, 62, 65, 70, 71, 74, 86, 109, 117, 123, 134
apples, 96
apricots, 15, 60, 92, 116
avocados, 133
bananas, 14, 41, 60, 79, 107
black walnuts, 103
blueberries, 112
brandy, 42, 88, 89
butterscotch/butterscotch chips, 14, 44, 82, 85, 91
caramel, 24, 98
carob, 14, 107, 108, 109, 110, 113, 114, 117, 120
carrots, 80
cashews, 60, 94, 116, 119
cherries, candied or maraschino/Kirsch, 42, 49, 58, 60, 69, 73
coconut, 15, 38, 51, 57, 60, 70, 72, 80, 83, 87, 91, 92, 94, 98, 110, 111, 114, 116, 119, 123, 133
coffee/Kahlua, 37, 54, 71, 99, 126, 132
cranberries, 127

cream cheese, 15, 46, 81, 85, 92, 100, 124, 130, 136
dates, 15, 60, 68, 96, 109, 116, 133
eggnog, 102
figs, 87, 116
fruit, candied, 134
fruit, dried, 15, 60, 87, 92, 116, 119, 136
graham crackers, 15–16, 63, 76, 82, 127
granola, 76, 110, 114, 116, 120
honey, 16, 76, 77, 84, 94, 104, 106, 107, 108, 109, 110, 113, 114, 117, 118, 119, 120
jam/jelly, 90
lemon, 16, 87, 95
lime, 83
macadamia nuts, 36, 60, 83, 133
malted milk, 59
maple, 16, 72
marshmallow, 16, 38, 56, 58, 60, 63
mincemeat, 88
mint/Creme de Menthe, 30, 124
molasses, 34, 82, 88, 112
oatmeal, 68, 107, 119
orange, 27, 34, 60, 65, 68, 81, 110, 118

peach, 136
peanuts/peanut butter, 16, 26, 40, 75, 79, 90, 91, 100, 108, 114, 116, 120
pecans, 24, 35, 38, 42, 44, 51, 53, 56, 66, 85, 98, 106, 107
pineapple, dried/candied, 42, 60, 80, 123
pistachio nuts, 52, 73
poppyseed, 95
pumpkin, 84
raisins/currants, 15, 28, 34, 42, 57, 73, 80, 82, 87, 88, 95, 96, 102, 103, 112, 114, 116, 118, 127
raspberries, 33
rum, 57, 61, 73, 102, 123
sesame seeds, 104
sour cream, 23
strawberries, 33
walnuts, 28, 41, 48, 56, 57, 58, 67, 68, 72, 80, 82, 87, 88, 95, 96, 99, 102, 103, 107, 112, 127, 136
whiskey, 99
white chocolate, 15, 43, 58, 62
yogurt, 32
zucchini, 28

Lisa Wolfson Tanner was born in 1957 in Los Angeles, California. Her artistic ability and desire to excel as an artist started in early childhood, as did her love for creative cooking and good eating. She has a Bachelor of Fine Arts in Illustration from California State University, Long Beach, where she excelled in her chosen field, making food illustration her specialty.

Lisa still lives in the Los Angeles area, where she is a very busy wife, and mother of toddler Jessica. She teaches art classes, is a free-lance illustrator, and enjoys jogging for exercise and relaxation.

For Lisa, *The Brownie Experience* is the beginning of many books to come.

Photograph by Paul Tanner